THE
BAREFOOT MEDIUM

▼

LETTING SPIRIT IN... ONE STEP AT A TIME.

For information regarding permission contact Emma Smallbone
via barefootmedium.com

Printed in the United States of America

First Publication, 2015

Paperback - ISBN 978-0-9947941-0-9

Ebook - ISBN 978-0-9947941-1-6

Cover & Book design by Morgan Rose

▼   ▼   ▼

I first met Emma in 2011 when she attended a workshop I held at the Galt first Spiritualist Church. From first meeting her I loved her enthusiasm, passion and drive - she reminded me of the Freddie Mercury song "Nothing can stop me now". Emma is very sincere, and loves making contact with the Spirit world, this enabling people to have emotional closure after the loss of a loved one and bringing also , the knowledge that their loved ones can continue their lives in a parallel sense, and that when physical life ends we will all be together again with those we have loved. This is a truly great gift to have. Emma's enthusiasm is , as was my own when I first discovered the variety of my Spiritual gifts, contagious and I am sure she will bring much joy to the many people she gives readings to, as well as her public work. Having met Emma on many occasions I feel sure her respect for her Spirit guides and communicators will ensure she will be able to help people for many years to come.

The world needs more people like Emma who are fearless in their wishing to establish the truth that there is no death!

— Minister Val Williams.

This is a MUST read for anyone looking for answers in their own lives or in the loss of someone they love. Emma beautifully entwines her own journey with the lessons she teaches her audience in how we too, can connect with Spirit. Take the journey with Emma, I know you will fall in love with her just like I did.

— Marnie Kay, Founder Meraki House Publishing.

▼   ▼   ▼

THE
BAREFOOT MEDIUM

▼

To all the loves and lights in my life.

To my dad for giving the gift of forgiveness and determination.

To my mum for being the strongest woman I know and for letting me "talk to Spirit" from day one.

To Bill for truly being my knight in shining armour and for putting up with me when no one else would.

And to my son for helping me see all the magic in the world again.

▼

Dear Friend,

First of all, thank you. Thank you for deciding to come on this journey with me. It took every ounce of courage I have to bare myself in the following pages in the hopes that you can learn something from it. That is the true purpose of this book and every session I deliver, to leave you with more than you came with.

So I want you to know something before we get started. I want you to know how special and magical you are. I know you don't always feel this way because, neither do I. We are so much the same, you and I. Yet, entirely different too.

I also know you think you can't do what I do. To be completely honest, for most of my life I didn't think I could do what I do. Until I learned I was already 'doing' it, just not altogether aware or very good at it.

I'm talking about letting Spirit in.

I know you are capable of doing what I do everyday. I know you are connected to Spirit, just as I am. You have been connected all along. And before we go any further, I want to show you how I know. It's what I call the Deja Vu Truth. You see, you think it's just a funny feeling of familarity, something you had a dream about or a place you have been before. You can't quite put your finger on it, it's just a fleeting moment of 'what the fuck?'.

The truth is, it's much bigger than that. I believe that Deja Vu is Spirit stopping you in your tracks, beaming you in to the present moment to pay attention.

Well, what good is that? Honestly, what purpose does that serve?

Understanding this 'truth' means you are one step closer to what I feel as an empath and a medium. I believe Deja Vu is Spirit telling you that you are in the exact place you are supposed to be doing the very thing you are supposed to be doing at the exact time you are supposed to be doing it. Perfect alignment. What an amazing gift!

Let's put it to the test! The next time you have the feeling of Deja Vu, stop. Take note of what is around you...

Is there a person there that you need to have a conversation with?

Is there a book you need to read right in front of you?

Is there a poster for a class you need to take?

Pay attention in that exact moment and take in everything around you as I will instruct in Chapter 1. The more you practise this connection in the moment with these subtle feelings, the easier it will be for you to connect with Spirit- like I do. From this moment on, I want you to believe. I want you to believe in magic and I want you to believe anything is possible. Pay attention, because I think Deja Vu is a signal that Spirit is trying to connect. Most of us just aren't listening.

So, start listening. Let Spirit in... One step at a time.

Love & Light,

CONTENTS

▼

THOSE
WHO DON'T
BELIEVE IN
MAGIC
WILL NEVER
FIND IT.

- ROALD DAHL

INTRODUCTION:
BORN BAREFOOT AND FREE.

I believe my purpose is to teach you how to believe in the magic I have always known. You may never see it as clearly as I do – but we believe in things we can't see all the time, so why not this?

My name is Emma Jane Smallbone. I was born in Portsmouth, England in 1976, on the 27th day of February, narrowly avoiding the day of leaping while landing on the day my older brother, Richard, was born just three years earlier. He was thrilled, I'm sure.

Up until a few years ago I was happily living with Bill my soulmate, working as a top ranked photographer, mother to the most amazing son, lover of all-things-cheese, and if you passed me on the street you probably wouldn't look twice save for the colourful tattoos and prominent lip piercing. What you wouldn't see is the secret I had been carrying with me all my life. A secret, that until today, I ignored, buried and avoided. For many years I truly misunderstood my purpose, leaving me confused with what was an uncommon gift, encapsulated in a fairly common exterior. I was lost and alone in my own world of magic.

I have seen Spirit my whole life. Until I was 8 years old, I thought everyone did. But it wasn't until a few years ago that I realized I could communicate with them in a way that would profoundly impact other's lives. I don't claim to be special, in fact, for most of my life I felt anything but. I do know, however, that I see things differently than most.

I knew I wasn't like everyone else. I just didn't see until now, that this was my strength and that one day, I would help a countless number of people all over the world with it.

Let me start by saying I don't like boxes. Especially ones I've been put in for the purpose of classifying who or what I am. However I understand the need for clarity and sometimes a label can communicate more effectively than I can. So today, I refer to myself as a medium and an empath. As a medium, I can see, hear and feel dead people, or as I like to call them, Spirit. I am a messenger, between the world you know and the Spirit world of our ancestors, able to communicate with both worlds simultaneously to deliver messages. I help people experience the truth, which is that life and love is everlasting. Beyond death we continue to exist in Spirit connected to this big beautiful world and everything in it. More poignantly, I provide closure and comfort to those looking for answers beyond the physical realm, beyond themselves.

It has been said many times that we are Spirit, having a physical experience. I am here to bridge the gap between what you believe now and this ultimate truth, demonstrate the existence of Spirit and prove our connection to that which we are. By engaging you in the world I have come to know intimately, I hope to raise your belief in the world of magic or Spirit, as I will refer to it from now on.

Along with my mediumship ability comes a heightened sense of emotional awareness. Meaning, I feel emotions in a big way. I feel your loved ones emotions- their energy so much so, that it affects my physical being. I can feel your emotions too, which comes in handy when your not 100% sure of who is coming through or the message you are receiving. I feel when you get it. When the clarity of the message hits home it runs through me like a giant shiver. This is why I do what I do. There is nothing more magical than all the emotions we can feel in this existence. I would never give up experiencing a father's pride for his daughter, you're instantaneous connection to a message and the most amazing feeling of them all, eternal love.

My wish is for all of you to feel it too.

I believe everyone is born with varying degrees of "gifts". Whether it be Clairaudient (the power to hear voices of Spirit or people who have passed on), Clairsentient (a form of psychic intuition) and Clairvoyant (the power to see beyond the physical) or even precognition, meaning foreknowledge of an event. Some people show signs at an early age, like my son. At 4 years of age he let me know that he was pulling cards for the invisible man shortly after one of my clients left one day. "Oh thats nice" I said, thinking 'Yep! That's my boy!' (Bill, comprehending what he said, shoots a wide-eye look my way.) Or the time that my boy wandered into the kitchen and just simply said... "Mummy I just saw babies with wings in the trees." Age 3. I love our family.

Others begin to develop their gifts at a later stage in life when they begin to look for some sort of purpose or something greater than themselves. It is a Spiritual journey we are on after all. My journey is to inspire Spiritual expansion in this world. I've learned along the way that this had to start with me. I had to make decisions to allow Spirituality into my life, or rather, take away all the stuff that was blocking who I really am.

▶   **What do I do?**   ◀

I give you what you need, not necessarily what you want.

While most mediums have some psychic ability, I cannot tell you next week's lottery numbers or who is going to win the Superbowl next year. However, I can communicate with Spirit which is evenly present at all times, meaning I can tap into what is known by the energy of the afterlife. For example, I can tell if you're a meticulous gardener or if your work desk is messy. Not because I can see it for myself, but because what Spirit sees – I see.

What I want to share with you first and foremost is that the messages I have for you are not always what you want but instead what you need to hear. Now, this can seem frustrating to some who are looking for a specific answer to a problem they might be facing (even I would like to know what day I'm going to retire and sit on a beach in perpetuity). But we have such a narrow version of our own experience, we only see what we want to see.

I help communicate between here and the afterlife. And I like to be barefoot when I do it. It's not necessary for me to connect but it's my thing. With my shoes off, feet on the floor or ground, toes wild and free, I feel grounded and purposeful; ready to give you my whole self as the vessel through which Spirit can communicate with you. It is also my sign to Spirit that I am ready to work. In doing this, I am able to share with you messages from Spirit to help provide a bigger picture or different perspective, encourage you to see what you need to see or pay attention to what you might be missing at any given time. Spirit just gets this shit. And I've learned to trust it, even when I think my mere 39 years in this physical body might know better. My ego has been checked a few times to say the least!

One of the biggest lessons I have learned is that the message Spirit is giving us will lead us to the answer we want. From my experience, Spirit is our guide and life experience is our teacher. In order to learn we must experience.

In my own life experience, my exploration of self and my connection to Spirit, I have come to learn some valuable lessons that I want to share with you in the following pages.

1. Magic is real so start looking for it

2. Your shit helmet is holding you back

3. Our feelings and emotions are like a compass. Follow them.

4. Your gut knows your true path

5. Finding your purpose is a journey

6. Timing is everything

7. STOP looking for a big sign, its not coming.

8. Choose happiness

9. Communication is everything, especially with yourself.

10. What if death isn't the end?

You might be wondering what all these lessons have to do with being a medium and an empath. The answer is perspective. While perspective may seem insignificant, it is anything but. Every class, session, event or one-on-one I host is an opportunity for me to provide you with a different perspective. A perspective that might just alter your reality, provide clarity and move you forward on something that had you stuck. You might not know why you are stuck. Spirit does. And it's my job to pass on the message to help you get unstuck, out of your shit-helmet and on with the wonderful life waiting for you.

▶ **What do I believe?** ◀

I believe we are all capable of many wonderful things. I believe that we are however, asleep to our true potential. There is a greater energy than what we can see. And I believe that because I believe, I can see what others cannot. Not because I am special, simply because I allow it in my life. I know that Spirit, our loved ones who have passed on are all here to guide us, they are rooting for us to live our best possible life. If you pay attention you will see the signs of their guidance, their messages and their love.

I know we are here to evolve, to grow and expand in ways we may not yet be aware of. There is purpose to everything, our passions, our pain, even a stubbed toe! Our job is to listen. If you could walk a day in my Barefoot-Medium-life, you wouldn't ever question that we are surrounded by those who have left this world, those we love and those who remain to guide and teach us in our own journey of fulfillment and connectedness to Spirit and each other.

I want to take you on a journey. A barefoot journey into the world of mediumship, in the hopes that you are inspired to explore the magic that exists in your own life.

I believe you have it within you to feel what I feel even if you may never see it physically, hear or sense it the way I do. Your own true potential lies in the beautiful synchronicity of life; the chance meeting, the whispers in the wind (or your gut) and the tingly goosebumps that are your own messages, your own level of communication with Spirit.

It took me a long time to accept that this is my place here, to share this gift, to allow others into the beauty of awareness and to teach the simple techniques I used to unlock my purpose. When you can learn this for yourself, I promise you'll appreciate the full cycle of life from which we come and that which we are destined to return to- the sacred energy of the universe. Where we came from we shall return, but while we are here let's get something straight...

'We are not human beings having a Spiritual experience.
We are Spiritual beings having a human experience.'
—Pierre Teilhard de Chardin

Meaning, you are magic. You are everything you need to be and more. So let go. Love yourself. Forgive yourself. And choose to be happy!

I did and I wouldn't change my life for the world.

Welcome, to the evolution of The Barefoot Medium.

Once you open yourself to Spirituality, you realize everything
is possible.

Creating your world takes Courage!

WE LIVE
ON A BLUE PLANET
THAT CIRCLES AROUND
A BALL OF FIRE
NEXT TO A MOON THAT MOVES
THE SEA
AND YOU DON'T BELIEVE IN
MIRACLES?

– ANONYMOUS

MAGIC IS REAL
SO START LOOKING FOR IT.

Now don't get me wrong. I'm not all 'woo woo' witchy woman here. I'm a science girl at heart with a nagging thirst for knowledge of how things work. This is where my interest in the world came from- the origin of which, science is still exploring. While I like to understand how things work, I never looked for the explanation of the one truth I have always known.

I have always believed that there is an energy that we are all connected to.

It just makes sense to me. We are energy! Molecules bumping up against each other. There is no doubt that our physical bodies have energy inside them. It is what keeps our heart pumping and our minds processing our thoughts. It has been proven that you cannot destroy energy. So, the only difference between us and Spirit is a solid mass, our physical bodies. When we die our Spirit (soul, consciousness, thoughts and memories) still exists. It is this energy that I tap into as a medium. I slow my own thoughts down to allow your loved one's memories and thoughts to enter my mind. It is a complete stream of consciousness, all connected. What is often referred to as the Universe, Mother Nature, God, and so on, I simply call Spirit.

When I step into the energy of Spirit I feel what they are feeling, see what they are seeing and hear what they are saying. All through a transfer of energy. What could be more scientific than that?

This energy that surrounds us is also the essence of who we are. The guidance we look for in our darkest moments is at our fingertips, in disguise or hidden behind our own veil of fear. It took me many years to trust that this energy was accessible to me for a purpose. I had always seen things that others couldn't see, felt things that others didn't feel. My life wasn't a journey of learning that it exists, instead it was a journey of trust, understanding and acceptance. Mostly of my own self.

After years of depression, anxiety, anger and a few nervous breakdowns, I was forced to face one thing. I had a gift. The Spirits that were showing up for me were here to guide me to do more. What if this was more than a cool party trick, more than just knowing they are here? What if it was a gift I could share with the world and in turn, help people in their own lives with it?

This question led to my decision to learn, to grow and accept myself as I am, embrace my life as a medium instead of fighting it. I now just know. Any doubts of my purpose are long gone, washed away with the decision to just be me. I realized I didn't need to force anything to be myself. To be my most confident, happy self I just had to decide, listen and allow. I just had to let Spirit in. And here I am.

It saddens me that most go through life not knowing, and that for so long I didn't want to know. But this is the journey we all must endure to discover our own truth, our own sense of knowing who we are and what we are capable of.

From a very young age, Spirit has shown up for me. In the beginning I just thought everyone saw what I saw. That idea was swept away with one fateful game of hide and go seek where I suddenly realized, everyone else didn't see Spirit like I did. I was eight years young on one of our many trips back to England with my parents and my brother to visit our extended family. We would all gather regularly at my Uncle Peter's 14th century home called The Neptune, situated in an old navel town in Suffolk. I know it sounds like a creepy set-up ripe for a ghost story but The Neptune wasn't just a place for people to stay, it was my family's home, and a playground for my brother and I. It was the coolest place to visit.

One night at The Neptune, the parents were preparing dinner for the entire family and all the kids including me, my brother and our cousins were sent off to play. The game of choice for us was usually hide and seek (especially at The Neptune) and today was no different. My cousin Oliver, as usual, yelled that the game was

This was the moment I realized that I could see Spirit and other people couldn't.

about to commence and as usual I was one of the first to get away. I ran off into a dark, corner room where I was sure I would be one of the last to be found. It was decorated with a bunch of old dusty furniture as my uncle (amongst other things) was an antiques dealer. The room was lit enough that I could make my way around it all but that was about it. I can still clearly picture the large mirror leaning against the wall and the old wooden four poster bed. I wasn't sure if I was allowed to be in there so I quickly hid under the old bed frame in the centre of the room, waiting for the inevitable 'seeker' to arrive.

All of a sudden this strange-looking kid dressed in weird old-time clothes came into the room. I didn't recognize him as someone I knew but it wasn't uncommon for some of my uncle's eccentric friends with their wandering kids to swing by at any given time. I didn't really think anything of it.

But, I could see that this boy wasn't like me.

He appeared different mostly because of his odd clothes. He was wearing a pair of knee-length grey wool shorts and a dark grey wool jacket with large black buttons holding it in place. He had short dark hair sticking out at the sides of the little cap he wore on his head. He looked like a little boy out of the movie, Oliver Twist. He seemed about my age or slightly younger and was really thin, sort of quiet in nature, respectful but friendly at the same time.

I gestured for him to come and sit down beside me and hide with me while I waited for the seeker. We chit-chatted for a bit discussing nothing really important but I felt safe with him, like he was my friend. After sometime (it did take them a while to find me as I expected) my cousins burst into the room screaming 'Found you Emma!'. As I climbed out from under the bed impressed with my clever hiding spot I noticed not one of them acknowledged my new friend, who was right beside me.

This was the moment I realized that I could see Spirit and other people couldn't.

Up until that moment, I had thought everyone could see what I saw. My mother certainly played along for years, always offering to push my imaginary friends in my imaginary pram when my arms got tired. I just thought she saw them too.

When my cousins came bumbling into the room and didn't even glance at my strange-looking friend who was sitting right beside me, I knew. I looked at this gentle young boy stunned and confused. He seemed to be invisible to my cousins yet I could see him as clearly as I could see them. He seemed to understand my concern and my silent question 'why cant they see you?' and in response, just shook his head from side to side, as if to say 'no, only you.'

And that was the beginning. I've always acknowledged Spirit as it shows up around me and they've showed up for me most of my life, even when I was pretending they weren't there. It's not a scary feeling or overwhelming by any means. It's actually completely normal for me, I always just acknowledged and moved on.

I guess it is so normal for me because nobody ever said 'shut that off'. They have always been a part of my life, I just controlled how much. Because of this awareness, I have always paid attention to what's happening around me, what people say and the energy I could so clearly pick up from the environment I was in. Whether I knew it at the time or not, I was paying attention to things that most people don't. I truly believe this is why I see what I see today.

▶ **PAY ATTENTION TO WHAT YOU ARE DRAWN TO.** ◀

I believe we all have an innate sense of what we are here to do, learn and become.

Where we are pulled in life, what we are drawn to is guiding the way. The things we instinctively like, our interests and what energizes us are signs pointing to our path and our purpose. We are all drawn to certain things in life. We all have passions, things we love to do, places we love to go and ideas or visions for our future- what we want. Pay attention to them, all of them. These are signs guiding you to your pure potential, your place of simply being.

My signs were loud and clear. Nature, photography, teaching and ancient knowledge.

As a child, my parents struggled to get me to come inside the house most nights. I loved to be in and around nature. I was always finding wounded animals and rescuing insects from impending doom. My first friends were the animals and the trees, I would talk them and they would talk back to me. They seemed drawn to me too. To this day, I get messages or signs from them when I'm paying attention. I thrive in nature, feel at home with the calm of the trees around me and the earth's strength below me. My bare feet, entwined in the dirt, connected at the core of my body. I feel alive surrounded by the natural beauty of the planet we live on, the divine energy we are connected to and the ever-present Spirit that flows through us all.

When I started learning about how the universe worked and that there was a higher energy, it started to make sense why I felt such a connection to nature. I craved it, I felt as if I was communicating with the earth, the trees and the animals. I was drawn to it and it is very much a part of my life today, everyday.

I was drawn to the arts, photography in particular. I loved inspiring beauty form behind the lens and capturing images, to preserve an experience or a feeling. I think it was a way of capturing everything I could feel as an empath, the emotion, the love, the fear- all of it. And I always found myself in a position where I was teaching others. I even became a photography teacher, unintentionally.

Ancient knowledge always fascinated me. I loved history and philosophy, reading and hearing stories of pagan culture, witches, wizards and vikings. Fantasy and reality all muddled into what we believe exists. It fascinated me. So much so that I drew people and experiences into my life to fill the need for exploration. I wanted to believe that what was taught to me as 'fantasy' could be reality, to understand why I could see Spirit which was already fantasy to most.

All of these things that I was drawn to do and experience (photography and teaching), things that I loved (nature and woo-woo stuff), kept showing up for me in my life until I paid attention to them. And they will for you too. Save yourself some time and start paying attention now. They are showing up for a reason.

'Respond to every call that excites your Spirit.' — Rumi

▶ **PAY ATTENTION TO THE PEOPLE AROUND YOU.** ◀

I believe our families, the people in our lives are all here to teach us something. I think we have challenges within our families for the purpose of growth, understanding our own selves and in turn learning how to understand others as well. Our family is our biggest teacher of patience, love and compassion.

Some of my biggest lessons began with my family (I have come to think this might be the case for everyone, whether you believe that or not). I love them, each in their own way and I believe they were and continue to be everything they need to be in order to help me grow into the person I am now. My personal, professional and Spiritual growth didn't come without the pain that was necessary to push me in ways I probably wouldn't have chosen for myself. And for that, I am forever grateful.

My strength comes from my mother, Judith. My mum is one of the strongest people I know. Growing up in the south of England, she was the only girl, and the youngest of three older brothers, Peter, Andrew and Vincent. A tom-boy by trade and a princess at heart, she was an explorer full of wonder and courage. I pretty much followed suit. With a long line of strong women, so did she. Her mum was a nurse working in London amidst the horror of World War II and her Dad, a driven salesman so the lust for a full life was in the blood. They moved around a lot as kids, she was always the new girl in town and this usually landed her in some hot water, she was a fiery young girl and still is, just like me.

My mum encouraged me to read as she herself had a huge thirst for knowledge. She didn't finish high school until later in life but she has always had a knowing and common sense beyond her years. She was always willing to teach it all to me. And encouraged my connection to Spirit by playing along, being a part of it, cementing my belief at a young age.

She met my dad, Fred when she was very young and had my brother, Richard when she was just 16. They were married that year and I was born three years later. My family shared two birthdays each year, my brother and I on the 27th February and my parents both on May 25th. Fun and frustrating at the same time. But we made the most of it usually doing what Richard wanted because I liked to hang out with the older kids anyway. When we were kids, Richard and I were inseparable, we might as well have been twins.

We played in the woods together in Denfield, a small town north of London, building tree houses and forts every chance we got. I have very fond memories of our time together, even after our pre-teen awkward phase. Our family moved to Canada when I was three to pursue work for my father at a time when Canada's industrial scene was in rapid growth.

Our travels back home to England as kids was often just the two of us on a jumbo jet to spend time with the family while our parents stayed and worked in Canada. In the old hotel owned by our grandparents, we used to run around the halls screaming and playing only to get in trouble and consequently- relegated to the basement to fold sheets and towels. Even though folding was punishment, it was fun. Our imaginations would run wild as we talked for hours on end while doing our chores.

My brother, Richard has always been an artist. He is incredibly talented. Which made growing up in the older sibling's shadow really hard for me. I was always known as 'Richard's Sister'. When our family and teachers realized I couldn't draw like my brother, I could smell the disappointment. Probably why I chose photography.

My dad was the disciplinarian. He was always the strict one out of my parents. One of the hardest working people I know, he very rarely took a sick day. He was a scientific instrument maker by trade, worked long hours coming home to eat a meal with the family, usually some sort of meat and veggie, then went to bed early only to rise early again for the next day. He liked order and regiment. He was the polar opposite of the creative wild creatures that he was living with. He probably didn't know what to do with my mum, my brother and I. He was a good dad. Loving when he needed to be and strict when we got out of line. Although, I didn't have this perspective until a few years ago.

He was an avid Philatelist, which is the fancy name for a stamp collector, winning gold medals and all. He was a blacksmith, a beekeeper, a gardener, motorcycle enthusiast. The list goes on. It is likely that I inherited my ambition and work ethic from him.

It may only be in retrospect that we appreciate the gifts we are given from the relationships within our families. My greatest challenge growing up was my relationship with my father, who I've realized I am a reflection of in many ways. That relationship was also my biggest gift in which I learned strength, independence and forgiveness. I am grateful for the experience he provided me in this life, I wouldn't be who I am today without it.

Pay attention to the people closest to you, and the part they have played in who you are today. What can you learn from them and your experiences with them? Life experience is your greatest teacher.

► **PAY ATTENTION TO HOW YOU FEEL.** ◄

How you feel is everything. It's your internal guidance system to light the way. More commonly known as your 'gut', your intuition is the special gift you have to tap into the world's energy and listen to the guidance it provides. It's all there waiting for you.

I know you've had that gut feeling. To stop, to start, to walk away. Your intuition guiding you on the path you need to be. But we don't always listen. Sometimes we think we know better. Sometimes we listen to the voice in our heads instead. Or the voices outside our heads coming from other people.

But your intuition always knows. It's always right. Think of how many times you have said to yourself 'Gah! I knew that was going to happen!' We know more than we think we know. We have an internal knowing, a feeling that if you pay attention to it, it can be very helpful in learning what we need to learn sooner and avoid the same mistakes over and over again. If we listen to it. If we pay attention to that feeling and what is going on around us.

THE BAREFOOT MEDIUM

16

There were many times in my life where I missed these signs. I believe we all do. Clouded in some fear, some habit and the big 'shit helmet' we all throw on and walk around in. It's the comfort zone. A shitty comfort-zone helmet of certainty.

There were three distinct times in my life where this shit helmet blocked my view. Impeded my vision, clouded my head and slowed me down. I wasn't paying attention to how I was feeling and I was living in my head with all the nasty thoughts swirling around about why I was stuck. College was one of those times for me. I was depressed, struggling in school and after a Spirit 'party trick' gone wrong, I shut Spirit out. I turned it off and blocked communication access with it. So much so, I was slightly worried I may not be able to turn it back on. I had fully committed to my shit helmet.

The truth is, I probably needed to be in that place for a while. I needed to have a really bad time so I never wanted to go back to feeling that way. And I did. It was a time where I found some boundaries, I learned to really not care what people think and learned a lot about my self without the presence of Spirit. I was stronger when I let Spirit back into my life because of it.

The shit helmet is a dangerous place to be. But if you know you're there, you can get out. Awareness is the first step to making the decision to change.

You have to know where you are before you can set the GPS to where you are going.

Believe me, I still have my moments! But now I have the awareness and the strength to stop, listen, connect with Spirit and pull myself out of the helmet. I simply learned to pay attention to how I feel. And you can too.

▼   ▼   ▼

EMMA'S EXERCISE • 1

▽

PAY ATTENTION TO THE MAGIC
OF THE PRESENT MOMENT

The magic is all around us. It's the moments of clarity, deja vu, tingly goosebumps- the moments when you think 'That's fucking weird!'. There are always signs pointing us in the right direction. Whether we choose to see them or not is our decision. The signs are everywhere! You have to really work at not seeing them. But we miss them so often because we are not paying attention in the moment. They could be things you are drawn to, the people around you, themes that keep showing up or physical senses or emotions.

Being an empath, many signs for me come from how I feel, physical senses and emotions I pick up. When I pay attention in the moment, I have one particular sign as a medium and an empath, to know if I am on the right track with a client or something I'm working on. It is a distinct tingle (like goosebumps) down my right arm. When I'm on the right track, goosebumps shoot down my arm like a wave.

The lesson here is to pay attention to the little things. The messages are there waiting to be decoded. Be present, in the moment and look around you. What do you see? How do you really feel? If you are ever experiencing anxiety or overwhelm, that is a sign you aren't being present. You are focusing on the past or the future. This takes away your power because you cannot change the past and the future has not yet happened. Stay where you have the power to do something, stay in the now.

Find complete awareness of the very moment you are in. Being present allows you to focus on this very second, on what is happening right now instead of your perception of the past of the perceived future. Be totally and utterly focused on the now.

I would like you to begin a new practice. The practice of being present, 'in the moment'. Here is how I do this daily:

- Put your feet on the floor. Hands on your lap. Now take 5 deep, controlled breaths.

- Draw in that breath all the way down to your toes. Feel it fill you up.

- Note the stress leave your shoulders. Note the texture of the floor under your feet.

- Feel your breath on the back of your throat as you control the flow of it. Breathe in for....1...2...3.... and out for ......1....2.....3.... and in for ....1...2...3.... and out for ......1....2.....3. Repeat this 5 times.

- Now for the next few minutes, try and take in everything around you. Notice what you touch How does it feel? See the light through the window or the trees and the wind on your face. What can you smell? Look slowly around you and take in everything you look at, appreciate its existence. This is where you find clarity. This is where the messages are.

You may not notice too much the first few times you do this, however the more you practise- the more you will allow into your awareness. You may even find some goosebumps along the way. Keep a journal on your 5-10 minute sessions and take note of everything you experience. Watch yourself grow in awareness. It's a beautiful thing.

'Wherever you are, be all there.' — Jim Elliot

LIFE
DOES NOT HAVE
TO BE
PERFECT
TO BE
WONDERFUL

- ANNETTE FUNICELLO

YOUR SHIT HELMET
IS HOLDING YOU BACK

We all have a shit helmet. Including me. I wore it proudly for many years, a big shiny shit helmet. You know, the kind that clouds your view, fogs your mind and blocks your creativity, compassion and love? I refer to it as a helmet to many clients, because I want you to know that you can take it off. You have chosen to put it on at some point for some reason, probably for protection or safety and have forgotten it was there. We just get used to the comfort and sometimes the attention we get from wearing a big shiny shit helmet.

I put mine on at a young age, I think to protect myself from seeing Spirit. Consequently, I really didn't have my life together for a long time. For the first 32 years of my life, I sucked at it. Sure, I come to you now with clarity, purpose and a vision for a grand future but for many years this seemed so impossible to me, from inside the helmet.

I was convinced that I needed to be like everyone else otherwise I wouldn't fit in. Yet my soul screamed for anything but. I felt condemned to chasing a life meant for someone else, believing this was the path to true happiness. I circled many different cliques looking for 'the one' that most closely resembled the largest part of me, only to find that I had become a chameleon in each, exposing only the part of me that fit so they were as comfortable as possible having me around.

I was living in pieces, never whole, to create ease for everyone else in my life.

After my first nervous breakdown, I picked myself up and pulled myself together enough to go to College. College was important to me, I wanted to be successful and more than that I wanted to learn how to turn my passion for photography into a career. It was all I wanted to do.

But I had had a difficult time keeping up in College. I failed all my theory classes, I failed English at the college level twice surrounded by kids who spoke English as a second language and they managed to pass. I had to take

I knew I was capable of something I was yet to understand. I think we all are.

extra classes and retake courses just to stay afloat. I had rifts with teachers, one in particular who all but failed me after a family portrait assignment where I handed in a photograph of my roommates and his boyfriend. Admittedly it was a poor shot, but it hadn't fazed me to think this might not be considered a family portrait– my roommates were a proud gay couple, yet I was given a '0' by the teacher for and I quote "no gender mixing". I don't know if his problem was with me or the family portrait of two men, either way I had to fight my way back into a passing grade with the college. Narrowly avoiding another round of that course for no reason.

I had no need to hand in work that was less than what I was capable of and yet I did. I had no need to have rifts with teachers and yet I did. I had no need to self-sabotage the career I wanted and yet I did. I was living in the shit helmet.

The only thing I could hang my hat on socially, was the cool party trick I had pulled from the closet, my mediumship. Realizing my friends found it cool to hear me strip down an unsuspecting recipient exposing their life's experiences and meaning, I began dabbling with it, seeing how far I could go. I really hadn't taken it seriously, I didn't even know I could take it seriously.

I knew I was capable of something I was yet to understand. I think we all are.

I had decided to live in residence for the first year to experience college life in the full. One night early in the year, I attended one of the floor parties which were notorious for a good time. We were all gathered around in one of the dorms having a good time and I hear someone yell "Let's watch Emma read Tina's palm!" Feeling slightly put on the spot but excited to demonstrate my trick, I eagerly obliged.

At the time, I knew enough about palmistry to know where the life line and marriage line were and that was all anyone really cared about anyway. But this time was different. As I took her hand in mine I felt like I knew more. Suddenly, I knew everything about her. It was as if I was living her life, it was so clear to me. I started speaking about specific things like the fact she had trouble breathing growing up, she was asthmatic. She was shocked. As a soccer player, no one knew this about her childhood. Apart from feeling slightly intrusive, I was having fun. For the first time in my life, I enjoyed having a gift that no one else could see but me. It became useful. I could do something with it, instead of just know that it's there.

I left it alone for a few months after that, in fear of being harassed all day to read my friend's palms. I didn't think too much of it until one night, I was encouraged again by my room mate to read her friend's palm, the way I had for Tina. I could tell she felt excited to hear what I had to say to her friend and so again, I obliged. This reading wasn't like Tina's. This time it felt much stronger. It was like someone was speaking through me, it wasn't me or my words. I told my room mate's friend about his entire life in great detail. So much information was coming out of me, like a waterfall I couldn't stop it. What came out of me next was so shocking that I knocked his hand out of mine and left the room in a hurry. I had told him how his life was going to end- that he would suffer from some sort of heart condition, more than likely a heart attack. He looked just as shocked as I felt. I couldn't believe I could allow those words to come out of mouth and I felt it shut down. I felt myself switch off the connection to this infinite knowledge in fear of saying anything like that ever again, much less knowing it.

I apologized immediately suggesting to the guy that it probably wasn't real. (I had no idea what I was doing!) Thankfully, he said it didn't really surprise him as most of the men in his family had heart issues. He said it was kind of comforting to know. I was unsure of whether he said it to ease my own distress or that he didn't really believe me, but I knew. I knew what I had told him and that I hadn't made it up. And I felt guilty for what I had divulged to him. If I had

had more control I wouldn't have let that information come out of my mouth. What good would it do him to know that?

That was it for me. I turned it off. It scared me that I lost control of what was coming out of my mouth and that it went as far as predicting how he was going to die. I think it was just as shocking for me as it was for him. With my mediumship shut off again, I focused on finishing school and moving on with life. Unsure of it's purpose in my life, I knew I didn't want it to be that.

Again, I had no real interactions with Spirit for quite a while. It was always in the back of my mind, Spirit was always there. I just chose not to communicate with it.

Until one night two years after I graduated, I was dating a poet. It wasn't altogether serious but he was 'boyfriend status'. From time to time he would get cold sores on his nose (not his lips which was weird) and he'd complain of how painful they were. When one of these cold sores would show up, he wouldn't leave his place until it was gone.

We were having a bbq in my back yard that evening and we were all getting ready to call it a night. It had just started to thunder storm. I went outside to breathe in the fresh air and the storm and I heard my grandmother on my mother's side whisper to me "cast a circle!" My grandmother was in a coma at the time, she was very ill and we knew it was only a matter of months before she might pass away. But I knew it was her voice. Even though I hadn't spent much time with her in my life, I had always felt a very deep connection with her.

I had seen the 'The Craft', and read enough books on magic to know what "casting a circle" was. I summed up some courage, and in my mind I cast a circle. In my head I called upon the sky above, earth below, fire within to help me move some of my energy. In that moment, it felt like my grandmother's Spirit entered my body and told me what to do. I walked right up to my boyfriend and gently tapped him on the nose. He jumped out of his chair and and yelled 'What the hell are you doing? What did you do to me?" I said "nothing" and walked away not really knowing what I had done.

What I did know was when I had touched his nose with my right pointer finger, it felt like a jolt of electricity went right through me, from my finger to my toes. It was as if I had electrocuted myself. In that instant, I knew I was reconnected with Spirit in a big way. I had never felt Spirit so close to me, alive within me. I was energized to bring it into my life. And all the beautiful synchronicity that led me to where I am today started showing up, on by one.

The next morning, the poet woke up and the cold sore on his nose was gone. Disappeared as if it had not been there only 12 hours earlier. I can't explain that one with science, but I thanked my grandmother for taking his pain away. And myself for realizing I had finally taken the shit helmet off. Sometimes we need a little help taking off our helmet. Sometimes we don't know we have it on. It was my grandmother who reminded me of the power I had forgotten. And now I can remind you of yours.

My grandmother passed a couple months after that. I know she has been guiding me in my journey towards mediumship. I feel her around me and often get messages from her. I wouldn't be the medium I am today without her.

▼   ▼   ▼

I never believed what I was capable of

EMMA'S EXERCISE • 2

▽

REMOVE THE SHIT HELMET AND TAKE A BREATHER. A POSITIVE SELF-TALK BREATHER.

The negative self-talk is only reinforcing one thing- that you have your shit helmet on. This shit helmet has been holding you back far too long. I know it feels safe in there where you can feel certain and sure of yourself but as long as you stay in there, the harder it is to come out.

It's time to take off the helmet, see yourself for who you really are, see the gifts that you have and celebrate them! So I want you to take your hands and feel for the helmet on your head right now. Picture it. What does it look like? What colour, size and shape is it? Now grab a hold of the base (if it's like an astronaut helmet) or the grill (if it's a football helmet). Take a deep breath in and yank it off your head!

Feel the freedom! See all the beauty in your life and all the magical colour and light that shines around you. Take another deep breathe and feel the positive, kind, peaceful words enter your mind.

Set the helmet aside for a little while and write this sentence out 10 times when you wake up and before you go to sleep everyday for the next week. And if you catch yourself thinking a single negative thought- STOP, remove the helmet, grab a pen and piece of paper and WRITE this sentence.

I am a beautiful, creative being, full of wonder for the courageous life ahead of me. I am love and light, and I choose to let Spirit in!

When you can become aware of your shit helmet self-talk, you can begin to change it. Before long, you'll become aware of when you are putting it back on, instead of when you need to take it off. Awareness is a beautiful thing- it can change your life.

NOTES:

NO ONE CAN
MAKE YOU FEEL
INFERIOR
WITHOUT YOUR
CONSENT.

– ELEANOR ROOSEVELT

OUR FEELINGS AND EMOTIONS ARE LIKE A COMPASS. FOLLOW THEM

For most of my life, I ignored my feelings. I focused on what everyone (school friends, family) wanted from me and based on the feedback, I thought I had to try and act normal, like they appeared to me. If life was the journey and my emotions were the compass, then being normal or fitting in was the destination. That was all I wanted in life, to fit in. The problem was that my emotions didn't point me in the direction of fitting in. I didn't know it yet, but I wasn't meant to fit in.

This is why I struggled for most of my life, I wasn't listening to my compass. We all have feelings and emotions for a reason. They are your compass guiding you in the direction you need to go. You need to listen to where they are directing you, you need to find YOUR destination. And like me, it may not be where you desperately want to go, but instead where you need to go.

Trying to fit in is like a one way sentence to a straight jacket. A mental straight jacket.

I never fit in. Ever. And believe me, I tried. Most of the time it was the usual gender discrimination as kids, trying to understand how we fit together; the girls didn't like me because I got along with the boys. And the boys never really liked me because I was just one of the boys. I was stuck in the middle, desperate for someone to like me, for somewhere to call my 'social home'. I did develop some friendships along the way- don't get me wrong here- I never had trouble making friends no matter how I was treated. I just never seemed to make the kind of friends that you keep for life and I craved a deeper connection.

I was one of the tallest kids in my grade, I liked to read and talk, express myself and communicate. In return I was teased

I had thrown the compass away. What good was it if it wasn't pointing me in the direction I wanted to go?

constantly, labelled stupid and fat. So, I either stayed home sick or stuck close by my brother, which I'm sure cramped his style and annoyed him to no end. I remember sitting by myself on the bus coming up with fantastic stories about how I was a beautiful princess, living on a new land where the King had to hide out, in fear that I would be kidnapped by the enemy! A wondrous fairytale I told myself to block out being called a freak.

If I was going to be different, I might as well be a princess!

Being one of the tallest, though, had its advantages. I was strong, I could jump the highest, knock the baseball out of the park. I was the kicker in soccer and I could throw the ball the furthest every time. I became obsessed with sports, I was good at it. Which ultimately reinforced the nail in the coffin on my social status. To the boys I was a freak (they were jealous) and to the girls- I wasn't like them (they didn't understand). Years went on this way and I became used to the constant teasing. I began accepting that I was different and ploughed myself into my strengths instead. Even with my sports skills, I still didn't fit in anywhere and desperately wanted to. I sort of learned to live with it as I think we all do. I developed a thick skin and just did what I loved to do. I guess I learned not to care what they thought of me. Probably a good trait to develop early on as a medium.

I don't remember much about high school, other than how I felt. I lived with a constant fog, a cloud of depression and anxiety hovering over me, while I squashed anything that caused me to be different from the other kids at school I so wanted to be like. I felt the pressure of my dad's expectations, never really being good enough for him, the shadow of my brilliant older brother and this nagging need to fit in somewhere. Anywhere, I didn't care. It was obvious at this point that I suffered from a learning disability, I struggled to remember anything that required my attention outside of my passions which were art and sports- two areas of school I felt I could just be me. I didn't like to memorize things that I didn't see any value in, math and english were boring to me and I abhorred the idea of being in a basic class so I forced myself into the intermediate and advanced classes putting all the more pressure on myself to keep up.

The beginning of a new chapter for me was when I moved to a fine arts school in London, Ontario. Bealart was like a haven for misfits. It was a magical place where art was coveted over any other subject. The arts department, where I lived and breathed was separated from the main school hall which allowed us to feel like we had our own little club. It was full of wonderful artsy things, tools, projects, paints, solvents and chemicals, so much so, I'm sure it would have burst into flames at the sight of a lit match. I was in Heaven. Finally, a place where I could see myself fitting in.

Then I met E.

I loved everything about him. I was completely fascinated with his heritage. His family were Native Americans and they practiced their beliefs daily. It was the first time I had been introduced to any kind of ancient rituals and an earth centred religion. It was just what I needed in my life. I began to understand that there were many different beliefs around the idea that there was something else beyond our physical world, yet it was somehow all the same to me.

What if I fall?
Oh but my darling,
what if you fly?
    — *Erin Hanson*

E accepted me for who I was. He and his family opened my mind to the idea that there is a whole bunch of shit out there (not just in books) that we know nothing about. Spirit was really active in my life at this time, they surrounded him constantly. I was always seeing figures in the corner or standing by my bed at night. They didn't bother me, they were just there and I kept quiet about it. Mostly in fear that he wouldn't really believe me.

E and I did everything together, we were explorers of anything and everything. Except for his extended fishing trips with his family up north every year, we were inseparable. I threw myself into this young love, thought it would be the forever-kind. Don't we all at the ripe age of 18?

Right out of out of high school, I wasn't accepted into College and just assumed I didn't need school to do what I wanted to do. I had become really good at photography. At a young age I had an eye for the shot and an ability to connect with the subject in a way that got the best out of them. So I went to work full-time at a photography lab. This is where I was most of the time if I wasn't with E. I had committed myself to learn everything I could about the art, the mechanics and the business of photography. I didn't love the job itself and my boss was awful but I loved the opportunity to immerse myself daily in my passion.

E had been away for the summer, on one of his extended fishing trips for which I patiently awaited his return. I usually wouldn't keep track of time and he would normally just show up when he got back. This time though, he didn't. The summer was ending and I still hadn't heard from him. I began to worry. Did something happen? Did he stay there? Or worse... Had he left me? E was my life, I couldn't bare the thought of him not being in it.

He didn't call, didn't write, didn't show up as he had always done. Nothing. I was crushed. I was angry. And I was confused. This was the catalyst that sent me into a spiral of negative emotion. The Shit Helmet was strapped on tight and it wasn't coming off.

I had thrown the compass away. What good was it if it wasn't pointing me in the direction I wanted to go?

Here began the first of three major breakdowns in my life. I had been living a basement apartment with no natural light (a mistake for me, I need nature) working a job where I was being treated poorly to say the least and now E had disappeared from my life. I was done for. I stopped leaving the house, barely getting out of bed each day to feed myself and I just felt lifeless. I became paranoid over the weeks, eventually installing a lock on the inside of my apartment without the landlord's permission- which is what tipped her off that something was really wrong, I'm sure. There was no need, she had an alarm system. I had given up on seeing E again, and I'd given up on myself in the process. The landlord, growing concerned about me (and likely her own property) phoned my parents. My parents called that day and said it was time to come home. I agreed.

In the middle of all of this, writing was something that helped sooth me- it was an outlet to express some of how I was feeling. I had always journaled but now it was on purpose. I knew I wasn't listening to how to I was feeling, I knew I was having trouble communicating with myself and this seemed to be the only way I could face how I was feeling and process it. I had no control over what I was thinking, I couldn't focus and all I could write was...

"This is what it must feel like to go crazy."

I was on a daily dose of Ativan, prescribed for the anxiety and placed into a support group for anger management therapy. I didn't feel angry, just sad and confused. I didn't understand why the doctors and the therapist I was seeing kept telling me that I was angry. It didn't make any sense to me, I couldn't feel anger, I couldn't feel anything. So I'd sit in the anger management classes surrounded by really angry people and just wait for my turn to talk about how I felt (which wasn't angry). Sure enough I'd be reprimanded for not accepting the anger that they were convinced I had.

Finally, I was home alone one day and just snapped, 'Ok I'm angry!' I'm going to go with this, I thought and so I stomped out the door to my parents backyard and hopped the fence into a farmers field. There I found one of those massive round bails of hay like a giant mini wheat. I don't know what came over me but I started punching. I must have stood there punching the shit out of the bail of hay for about 10 minutes until my knuckles were bruised and bleeding.

I guess I got it out of me somehow, from that point on I started healing. I didn't feel numb anymore.

What I realized years later, and I see it now as I help people heal, I think we are affected by energy around us. Some of us more than others. For myself, as an empath, I understand now how energy affects me not only from the physical world we live in but also the Spirit world. At that time in my life I was ignoring my connection to Spirit but that didn't make it go away exactly. I was still picking up the energy from Spirit and from people around me and because I wasn't understanding it all, it was fogging my mind.

This is part of why I do what I do now. I don't think there is one answer to help everyone when we are feeling this way in life, and I believe we all experience these emotions at different times for different reasons. We don't always need Ativan, or an anger circle or to punch a bail of hay. Sometimes we just need guidance, understanding and someone to say it's ok, everything is going to be ok.

Listen to your emotions. They are trying to tell you something. For me, it was that I needed to let go of the hurt I was feeling. The minute I allowed myself to do that, I had opened myself up to heal.

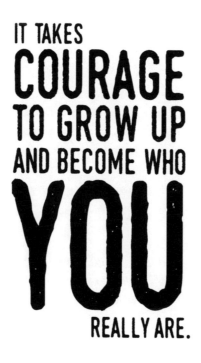

IT TAKES
COURAGE
TO GROW UP
AND BECOME WHO
YOU
REALLY ARE.

– EE CUMMINGS

EMMA'S EXERCISE • 3

▽

HOW DO I REALLY FEEL ABOUT THIS?
WHAT CAN I DO TO CHANGE IT?

Our emotions are our guidance system. Yet we tend to squash our emotions and bury them deep so we don't have to face how we really feel. Then somewhere along the line we emotionally explode and people wonder why the emotional outburst, all of sudden. When truthfully it was rumbling under the surface all along. We need to learn how to listen to our guidance system and what to do with what we find.

This is tough to do at first. Sometimes how we feel is buried deep under layers of lies and stories we've made up but there is beauty in connecting with how we are really feeling. There is honesty, integrity and authenticity. And when you face how you are really feeling, you can actually do something about it.

1. Think of something that has been bothering you, even if you aren't particularly upset or angry about it. Sit down with a pen and paper and write down how you really feel about it. As if no one is ever going to read it, how do you really feel about this bothersome thing? Keep going until you surprise yourself with the answer- then you know you've gone below surface level!

2. Then step away from the feelings you've written down. Think about what you can do to heal from it. Even if you aren't sure yet, what would be one step you could take in order to move forward? Then commit yourself to doing it.

We must express how we are feeling in order to be at peace with it. We don't always need to understand it, merely accept it and do something about it so we can move on. Failing all of that, find a bail of hay and go at it. Worked for me.

NOTES:

_____

_____

_____

_____

_____

_____

_____

_____

_____

_____

_____

_____

_____

• FEELINGS ARE YOUR COMPASS •

YOU
JUST HAVE TO HAVE
THE
COURAGE
TO LISTEN
TO IT.

YOUR GUT KNOWS YOUR TRUE PATH.

▼

Sometimes what we want, we aren't ready for. Sometimes what we need is to not have what we want, so when IT comes along we are the person we are meant to be – in order to keep it.

This is my philosophy around meeting Bill, the love of my life, my soulmate and the guy who Dances in his underwear like no one is watching to make me laugh. I truly believe, had Bill come along any earlier I would not have been the woman for him. The timing had to be the way that it was in order for us to work. It doesn't mean everything is perfect for us now however we wouldn't have ended up together any other way.

I believe this to be true for everyone and everything in our lives. If something you want isn't in your life yet, there is a reason. It isn't meant for you yet. And that's ok. Be patient, find your passion, your happiness within yourself as you are now and grow into the person you need to be. Whatever you want is on the other side of that transformation.

The things you want or desire will come when you are ready to receive them.

I'd had a couple of relationships in my life that were somewhat serious, most ending in heart-ache, and not one in which I could truly be my fabulous, funny, medium-self. I always felt like I had to hide the real me.

Prince Charming was nowhere to be seen, so this princess had to save her own ass.

I threw myself into my work as an assistant to an incredible fashion photographer and started to build my own life around my passion.

I had come to a point where I was completely happy being alone. For so long I had looked to others to make me happy, eventually I stopped looking for it outside and realized I could make myself happy. And so I did in my little bachelor apartment in the city of Toronto, just living and enjoying my life. I was living my dream assisting a prominent female photographer on major contracts for magazine cover shoots. I felt proud of what I had accomplished. All the ups and downs, the hard work had been worth it. I had set a goal and achieved it. I just loved my life. I had this bustling local pub I loved to eat at, I lived above a fantastic hairdresser who cut my hair for five bucks. I just had the perfect little set up and I can remember thinking, 'I really don't need anybody in my life to make it any better. This is good.'

Until one day, a friend unintentionally (I think) disrupted my contentment. We were out for a drink on a Friday afternoon catching up on life as we often did and she decided to bring up my single status as the next topic of conversation. She knew I hadn't really been serious about anybody for a while and well, this was probably as good a time as any to poke at it. Truthfully, anyone paying attention to my local pub visits and five-buck-cuts enough to notice I was in a lone-zone would probably have been more concerned about my life choices and the direction in which I was headed than I was.

That day, my friend casually asked me a question that changed the course of my life, "Aren't you lonely?" She asked. Caught off guard, I paused, pondering the intent of the question. "Not really, I don't really think about it much", I said, "I'm pretty happy with my life!" Unsatisfied with this answer, she proceeded with the next question..."Well, have you ever thought about who you might like to end up with?" Huh. I thought for a minute. "Well, actually... no. I've never had a dream guy in mind." That was the truth, except for a few physical traits I could think of, I really didn't know what I would want from someone. "Think about it," she said, "...might be a good idea to know what you want."

End Scene. Commence... a flood of new thoughts. I started to think about what she had asked me. So much so, I took to writing a list of all the things I would like to find in a someone.

That list went something like this...

- Needs to be taller than me!
- needs to be able to toss me across the room. Like a lumberjack. (I'm no small girl... but it would be nice to feel like one!)
- needs to be scruffy, ruff around the edges, manly
- needs to be handy
- Big lips are a must
- Intelligent
- Sense of humour

The last two have always been of particular importance to me, more than all the rest. But if I had come across any one of the above items, I'd have probably jumped in and maybe even been relatively happy, for a while. I guess I just hadn't really taken notice of my social status until it was brought to my attention that being alone may one day get lonely. Now, I couldn't help but think about my new found awareness of what I wanted.

This was the beginning of a personal transformation for me.

Two weeks later, one of my good friends invited some of her 'out-of-towner' friends to the city for the night. I hadn't met some of them before but we were all friendly and having a good time getting to know each other. We headed out after dinner to see Mooney Suzuki at the El Mocambo on Spadina Avenue at the edge of the bustling China Town in the heart of the downtown core of Toronto. Now, this particular group of friends (at least the ones I knew) were the type to be at the front of the crowd, pressed against the stage and enthusiastic about the hundreds of sweaty drunk people bumping up against them. I was the one in the group who would always stand at the back of the room and enjoy the show from afar, clean and dry, for the most part.

This night, was similar to most with this group of friends. They were up front as usual and I was doing my thing at the back of the room enjoying the show. The difference was, I wasn't the only one this time. Joining me, was one of the out-of-towner's that I had only briefly spoken to at dinner. Apparently he didn't like the sweaty back rub up front either. I found myself having an amazing conversation with this tall, handsome, manly guy named Bill. We sat on the pool tables at the back of the bar for most of the night completely engrossed in each other and the conversation. While everyone else was up front squashed against the stage enjoying themselves, Bill and I were at the back of the room getting to know each other, loving every minute.

Timing is a funny thing. Only in retrospect, does it make sense.

I remember thinking 'Wow! This guy is actually asking me questions and responding to what I am saying!' This wasn't like any other conversation I'd ever had with a guy. This one was different. Bill was interested in me and what I had to say. Refreshing. He was intelligent (Check!), 6 foot 5 (Check!), a tool and die maker (Check!). All of the things on my list. I was drooling. Here he was, the perfect guy right in front of me, as we hung out at the back of the Mooney Suzuki show for the entire night. I knew, that night I had met the man I was supposed to be with. I could feel it in my gut. And it made me nervous.

I called my mum that night after I got home. I told her that I had met the man I was going to be with for the rest of my life, Bill.

Now I don't think he realized that I liked him that night, and now knowing him, I know he is completely oblivious to any female attention. So it took me a good month and a half to get his attention and to have him come back to Toronto to see me. But I just knew I had to. And when he arrived I made sure he knew that I was 'the one', whether he was open to it or not at this point was irrelevant. I just knew.

We bumbled around for a bit, dating but in a weird friend-zone kind of way figuring it all out. Neither of us had even entertained anything serious for years in our own lives and here we were-facing something real and with some distance between us. He hated the city but I lived and worked there, so he begrudgingly visited. Secretly, I would have given anything to pick up and move to the country with him immediately but in the beginning I was hesitant in fear of moving too fast for him. It wasn't until New Years Eve of 2000 when we truly decided together, (not just me in my head) that this was it. We knew wanted to be together.

As I think about that now, it amazes me that a chance meeting (in a city of millions of eligible men) connected me with a man who was everything I wanted AND living in the countryside-where I needed to be. Magic.

This was a big bold decision on my part. This decision was me following my gut- leaving behind my career in the city, my friends and the life I had created, for the life I knew I needed to be living. Only months later, I made the decision to move to the country to be with him, whether he liked it or not. This is a large part of our relationship- I make wild decisions and he obliges when he realizes there's no deterring me. There was an adjustment period as we got to know each other after we moved in together but I never stopped knowing he was the one for me.

We started out awkwardly learning about each other's quirks, as most do. For me, this was the first time in a relationship that I needed someone to know everything about me, probably even to my detriment. He was much quieter than me, an 'under-sharer.' I'd have to pull information from him, not that he was hiding anything-he just didn't feel the need to talk a whole lot. While I compensated for the both of us, 'over-shared' almost obsessively. For the first time in my life, I felt completely myself and even slowly let him in on my Spirit world, which he seemed to accept.

For the most part I assumed he felt the same way about me that I felt about him based on the fact he was still around. But at some point, a year in or so, I realized this wasn't a sustainable plan for my emotional security (considering the impact of E's abrupt disappearance from my life), I needed some sort of commitment from Bill. So one day I nonchalantly suggested that he should buy me a ring, something that meant we were committed. I didn't need the whole wedding thing I reassured him, just a ring to feel like he was committed to me. He agreed, surprisingly. I was ecstatic! I became fixated on finding the perfect ring for myself. Which seems funny now that I think about it. I started shopping everywhere on and offline for the perfect ring for me, something earthy and unique. We browsed catalogues online at night and visited stores on the weekend. We traveled all over the countryside looking for little independent jewellers who might have something unique enough for me.

Nothing I found really wowed me until one day, a sunny Saturday afternoon, we wandered into a custom jeweller in a small town called Brantford. As soon as we walked up to the glass covered counter- I found it. "Oh my God, that's IT!" I yelled. It was a blue topaz in a white gold setting. I looked straight at Bill and said, "that's the one." Relieved I am sure, he pulled out his credit card and purchased this masterpiece we had been hunting all over the countryside for. It had to be fitted to my finger which they said would take a week and we were done! I skipped out of the store in love with this beautiful piece of jewelry that meant Bill was committed to me.

A week came and went, slowly, and we returned to the store to pick up the ring. I must have looked like a kid at Christmas sitting below the tree waiting for permission to open the gifts. While we waited patiently for the store clerk to retrieve the newly fitted ring, we were watching another couple decide on their engagement ring right in front of us. The sales lady had pulled a ring out of the case and given it to the man- the woman with him seemed particularly pleased at the sight of it. We watched the guy gently place the ring on the woman's wedding ring finger as they looked lovingly into each other's eyes. Bill leaned toward me and with a slight sense of panic in his voice, whispered to me... "Was I supposed to do something? Should this be fancier?" I didn't really know.

All I knew was that I wanted to be with him. I've always known that. I think we all have things in life that we know for sure. This was one for me.

I'd never placed much importance on being married and wedding photography probably played a part in that, but we still entertain the idea every now and then. I'm still not sure what this ring represents to both of us now, but at the time, it meant a symbol of his commitment to me. And I love him for that.

Timing is a funny thing. Only in retrospect, does it make sense.

There were many coincidences in my life leading up to the point of meeting Bill. Not the least of which being that I had actually met him five years earlier. I didn't know this until recently when I was going through an old photo book. I found a photo that I had taken at a friend's party and there's Bill, plain as day standing in the background. We were totally oblivious to each other at that time in our lives.

I've learned everything happens at the right time. The right time may not be your idea of the right time but if it hasn't happened yet, you may not be ready for it yet. Just like if Bill had met the me in the photograph, we likely wouldn't be together today. I had to grow into the person that he wanted to be with, and I had to be clear on the person I wanted to be with in order to identify him in the first place.

Divine timing isn't always obvious, until it happens. Now I just smile and know it was meant to be.

Meeting Bill and moving to the countryside to live in nature was one of the turning points in life. A catalyst in my becoming the person I was meant to be, who I am today. I became confident with him- he allowed me to be my true self, my whole self. I listened to my gut, my intuition for the first time in years and instinctively made decisions about myself and my life. I don't believe we always need someone to find this part of ourselves and I had somewhat made my own way toward this new level of self-confidence before I met him, but something unlocked when we connected. Something opened inside of me. I felt it, I listened and I stayed true to that gut feeling.

"You don't love someone for their looks, or their clothes or their fancy car, but because they sing a song only you can hear."
—Oscar Wilde

▼   ▼   ▼

EMMA'S EXERCISE • 4

$$\triangledown$$

WHAT AM I COMPELLED TO DO TODAY?

There will be many times in your life when you have this gut feeling. About people, a job or career, your lifestyle and everything in between. I believe this gut feeling, your instinct, is your connection to Spirit. And like I said Spirit just gets this shit. So listen to it.

Think back to some of the major experiences in your life, trace back the time and circumstances prior to the experience and you'll find you already had a feeling, a knowing - you just weren't listening to it. So start listening now. Have the courage to give it life, even if what it's telling you is scary. This is your intuition, your instinct guiding you on your path. If you're ever not sure of what to do, sit quiet for a few minutes and ask. Then, don't think- just feel. What do you feel? Which way are you pulled?

Do you ever feel compelled to do something? But your ego (brain/ common sense) takes over?

Do you ever get a feeling about a person you need to talk to or a place you need to go to?

Choose a day. Possibly a day off for your first few times and make all your decisions based on your gut. I bet it takes you somewhere magical.

I challenge you to start listening to your gut everyday. And listen less to your ego. When you feel compelled to do something, go somewhere or say something- do it. Don't hesitate.

Ask yourself as you begin each day, 'What do I feel compelled to do today?'

That is exactly how I ended up where I am today.

NOTES:

_____

_____

_____

_____

_____

_____

_____

_____

_____

_____

_____

_____

_____

_____

_____

· YOUR GUT KNOWS ·

THE
THINGS
THAT YOU ARE
PASSIONATE
ABOUT ARE NOT
RANDOM.
THEY ARE YOUR
CALLING.

- FABIENNE FREDRICKSON

FINDING YOUR PURPOSE
IS A JOURNEY NOT A DESTINATION.

Who you are today, isn't who you were a few years ago. What you started out doing in life doesn't have to be where you end up. So many of us are caught up in finding the meaning of life, but what if the meaning of life is the journey? The experience, the growth, the evolution of who we are. We all have themes, things that keep showing up in our lives until we pay attention and somewhere in there is that purpose.

Discovering our true selves is the first challenge, and when faced with that, acceptance is the next.

For me, it was always my mediumship. Looking back over my thirty-something years of seeing Spirit, I knew I was pushing aside the very thing I needed to explore. I just wasn't ready. And so, I found purpose in what I was doing instead, photography. I believed that being an empath and a medium enhanced my photography skills. I didn't realize it could possibly be the other way around. Photography is a big passion of mine, always has been, and I am really freakin' good at it. For many years, I threw myself into what I was good at and built a big business out of it in the process.

Since I was 15 years of age, every single spare moment I could find, I spent learning how to become the best photographer I could be. I consumed myself with it. Everything I ever did, school, college, part-time and full-time jobs all revolved around the art of capturing something in a still image. I attended Bealart (known as THE fine arts school) in London, Ontario then onto College for Commercial Photography, all the while working in labs, at camera stores, as the school photographer and as the lab technician in the photography department at school. I did it all and loved every single moment.

My life had become one big photography career. I was good at it. I enjoyed it and for those who were willing to work hard in the industry, there was a lot of money in it. I often wonder if it was a natural extension of my mediumship. As an empath, I could read people and emotionally influence them to expose their true energy to me, then capture it on film. I can build a strong sense of rapport with people, feel what they feel and connect in a way most people can't. I was capturing people's precious moments and loving every minute of it, whether it be a family portrait, new born baby, an event or a wedding. I got to experience everyones special moments from behind that lens.

After I moved to the countryside with Bill, I was convinced that I needed to work for myself. Really I just wanted the freedom to do what I wanted to do, so started doing some local photography work. I attracted some small jobs, portraits, a wedding here and there throughout the year. Everyone supported me, helping to find work for me, including my dad who had never really celebrated any of my accomplishments. He still didn't with my photography in the early days. At least not with words. I knew he approved and thought I was good at it as he referred me often, but I was always looking for the words. Maybe he didn't give them to me because inside I knew it wasn't my path either. I just went with it, and it came relatively easy to me.

It was at this time that the news broke within my family that my dad had betrayed my mum. This broke us as a family. I didn't need another reason to shut my father out of my life, but this made it easier to let him know that was my decision. I called him after I mustered up some guts, and let him know I did not want to speak to him or hear from him. I wanted nothing to do with him. And that was it. In my mind I had cut the strings that were holding me down. I had removed the burden of needing his approval, and I was free to find my own voice, my own approval and my own happiness.

"The secret of change is to focus all of your energy , not on fighting the old but on building the new." —Socrates

After I severed all ties, I ploughed myself into my business. I began promoting myself, actively building my photography business and referrals began flowing in effortlessly. Before I knew it, I became consumed with building a big business. It all happened fairly quickly, word of mouth spread and my calendar filled up with bookings. It grew from a few weddings and portraits in the beginning to over 25 weddings a year which is a lot! Avoiding Canada's winter months, that's almost every summer weekend! Eventually in my final year I clocked in at 427 portraits and 7 weddings. All I did was work, work, work. And stress, stress, stress over work. A cycle of stressful success. Don't get me wrong, I felt accomplished. I had achieved what so many photographers dream of. But I was working 80 - 90hrs a week for years upon years. I had employees and schedules and piled-up editing work, not to mention the administration side of things- my least favourite part of owning my own business. I was also teaching at the local college at this time. Which was another 'wartime' job. At one point, I was teaching 4 classes a week! On top of all my other work, I was beyond overwhelmed.

I just kept running on the hamster wheel until one day I woke up and faced myself in the mirror. Was all of this what I really wanted?

The answer was 'no'. I loved photography and I loved earning money but I knew in my gut it wasn't my purpose. It was a passion I was good at.

I think so many of us do this in life. Until we wake up one day down the road thinking 'what happened?' or 'What else is there?' Questions I faced at this time in my life.

These questions are good. And we should be asking them all the time. Because at one time, the business I had built was what I wanted. Everything I had, at one time, was what I wanted. And it's ok for what you want to change. In fact, I think it should evolve in your life in some way.

▼   ▼   ▼

EMMA'S EXERCISE • 5

▽

EXPLORE YOUR GIFTS AND FIND SPACE
FOR THEM IN YOUR DAILY LIFE

For a long time, I didn't allow myself to explore the gift I had been given. I had been blocking any purpose for it by not engaging in the joy it could give me to simply explore my connection to the Spirit world. I allowed my shit helmet to block what was a part of me all along. And because I didn't explore it, I didn't believe I really had a gift until I was jolted me awake with a new awareness. I could no longer ignore it. It was through these gifts that I found my purpose.

Ask yourself, what gifts are you ignoring? Whatever is stopping you from exploring these beautiful talents in life, isn't as strong as you think it is. But you have to make a decision to do something different. You have to make a decision to go for it, regardless of what anyone else thinks. Remember, they all have their own shit hemet.

• Write a list of three things that you are gifted at.

Can you sing? Can you do complicated math problems in your head? Can you fix anything without looking at a manual? Can you write? Are you athletic? Are you a great listener?

• Now have a look at all the gifts you have written down.

Can you identify a theme? Are they all about communication, technical skills, comedy, exercise, helping people?

• Make it a daily practise to include one or some of these gifts into your life. Enjoy the magic of your gifts even if only for a moment.

The things you love or are good at are not an accident, and by creating a space to enjoy them, like I did, you'll find a purpose for them.

Find a place for your gifts in your daily life and you'll watch your joy increase.

NOTES:

_____

_____

_____

_____

_____

_____

_____

_____

_____

_____

_____

_____

_____

PATIENCE IS THE CALM ACCEPTANCE THAT THINGS CAN HAPPEN IN A DIFFERENT ORDER THAN THE ONE YOU HAD IN MIND.

- DAVID G. ALLEN

TIMING IS EVERYTHING.

▼

Timing is everything. And not within our control most of the time. As much as we can make decisions and influence direction, I believe the timing of our lives is in the hands of the Spirit world. But we get nudges to help us along every now and then. I believe that every single one of our ancestors that came before us is standing right behind us pushing us to do better than they did. What parent/grandparent/uncle/aunt/brother/sister wouldn't want better for their loved one? I think they can look at our lives and see where we are headed. But it is up to us to pay attention to the signs and choose the path we walk. And everything that is in our lives is here for a reason. Even the timing of what shows up is for a reason.

For example, I had the chance to meet Bill five years earlier, yet I didn't. I believe I wasn't the person I needed to be then for us to work out the way we did. It had to happen the way it did. Divine intervention as it is sometimes called, the universe-saying 'Not yet!'

In the space of two months my life totally changed. Every decision I had been living with up until now, became the past and I started rapidly evaluating every single one. I began to think of my values as a guidance system, instead of my pain.

For most of my life, I had never really considered having a baby. I had actually told my mum once that I wanted to become a celibate nun- just so she wouldn't ask me about having kids of my own. I'm not sure why I revolted against the idea of having kids but I'm sure my nightmarish school experiences had something to do with it. Either way, I made the decision long ago that motherhood wasn't for me. I did have a vision though, when I was 16 I saw myself in the future, a grey-haired older woman living in a log home up on a hill with water near by, and a small blonde child who appeared to be mine. In the vision, I was watching fondly, as the child played outside in the forest. This is the most vivid dream I've ever had, I can still feel it. But that was it. After that, I was pretty much convinced that if I ever was to have a baby it would be a miracle baby. Or it would be a 'whoops baby', like my brother had been for my mum. I did everything I could to prevent having a baby from that point on. I even helped create a group in high school about teens teaching teens about sex ed.

I had also been diagnosed at the age of 27 with Polycystic Ovarian Syndrome, which is a condition affecting a woman's fertility and hormone balance and typically leads to cysts on the ovaries, irregular periods, weight gain along with depression and anxiety. PCOS affects about 1 in 20 women which is a larger number of women than most realize and essentially means I don't ovulate the way most women do. Instead of the eggs travelling down the fallopian tubes, mine turn into cysts on my ovaries and don't travel anywhere near where they need to be to make a baby. I had always had the extreme symptoms of PCOS so I knew that if I ever decided to become a mum, it was going to be a challenge.

At the time that Bill and I had made the decision 'no baby', my photography career was really taking off. So was my connection to Spirit. It became a nightly thing to see Spirit in our home and not just a couple but many and often. They would swirl above my head in bed.

More often than not, they were Spirits I didn't know until Bill's Dad, Cliff showed up. Cliff had passed away recently after a two year battle with ALS. I started to see him in Spirit, often standing in our closet at night as I moved around the room. He would grace our presence by sitting on the end of the bed, always with his back turned to us like he didn't want to intrude. I felt a strong urge to tell Bill, yet he was still grieving and we hadn't thoroughly explored my gift together yet. He knew what I had access to but I didn't know if he would believe me in this case or think I was just trying to console him.

At first, I thought that I might have been seeing him because I wanted to make things 'ok' for Bill. I so badly wanted him to heal and feel better. But, as Cliff began showing up often, I realized it was more than that. There was something else I was supposed to do.

As all of this was going on in our lives, I had a nagging feeling. Something deep down, urging me to explore this part of myself, this gift I had not yet fully opened, this gift that was beginning to force itself into my life, whether I like it or not. And I kinda liked it.

I began looking for answers. For the first time in my life I wanted to understand it better, explore it and learn what I was supposed to do with it. I sought out a friend of mine, Alex who introduced me to Reiki, a Japanese technique using your hands to heal. It is believed that Reiki allows the practitioner to transfer universal energy through their palms to encourage healing in the receiver. Alex introduced the idea to me that because energy is fluid, it could get stuck. This had never really occurred to me before, yet made total sense. I had felt stuck many times in life and each time I could trace it back to the block of energy. During my first session with him, I announced "Now, you may think this is crazy but I want you to move my mojo around so I can talk to dead people." He laughed at the idea that something might be weird to him. It was clear he wasn't fazed. Alex went to work on me and I immediately felt a shift take place. I felt like I could see clearer, it was a mental clarity like never before.

For the first time in my life, I began to believe... I had meaning and purpose.

For the first time in my life, I began to believe. I began to believe that this gift was more than a cool party trick, it had meaning and purpose. I had meaning and purpose. What a powerful realization.

This realization brought on many feelings. Calm, clarity, excitement and urgency. Urgency in a weird way. Urgency in my need to ensure this gift doesn't stop with me. I needed to have a baby, I needed to have a baby NOW before my time was up and that window with PCOS was closed, forever.

I sat Bill down one afternoon after I had carefully calculated the environment, timing and his mood for optimum results. I looked him in the eye and said, "Bill, I want to have a baby." He looked slightly confused as we had previously discussed this idea and both agreed it wasn't in the cards for us. "Are you sure?", he asked. "Yes. I'm certain, and it has to be now," I responded. He pondered for a minute, looked around, then back and me and said "ok then." I was shocked. That was easier than I thought. "Let's get to it!" I said. Once you start trying to make a baby, it's not as exciting as you think it is. At first it was like 'Oh my god! we are making a baby!', then after a while it sounded like 'Ugh do we really have to do this again?'. But I knew exactly when I got pregnant, Feb 13, the day before Valentine's Day. And about 2 weeks after we started trying. I just knew I was pregnant- I have always been that way with my body. It happened so fast, we didn't even get to tell anyone we were trying. When we sat Bill's mom down to tell her we were pregnant, she thought we were going to tell her we were getting married. I guess we aren't overly concerned with the tradition of things being in a certain order. I didn't care, I was the happiest I had ever been.

My body loved being pregnant. During those nine months I carried my son, I was probably the healthiest I have ever been too. I no longer had synthetic hormones in my body (to avoid any chance of pregnancy as I had wished for so long), I lost thirty pounds, all my PCOS symptoms seemed to disappear, I had tons of energy and I was really happy. In the beginning I slept twenty hours a day. I do not know how people have a job and carry an unborn child at the same time. I needed that sleep! When I wasn't sleeping, I continued to squeeze in my photography where I could, right up until I was eight and a half months along, shooting weddings and portraits with a giant belly and my camera sitting on top of it.

I researched EVERYTHING, as usual. As a result, I had decided to have a home-birth and so, we had midwives working with us all along, preparing us for the birth. At the time I had had a photography client, Jessica, who was well-versed in hypno-birthing, where you hypnotize yourself so as not to feel any of the pain associated with the birth of a child. I didn't hold onto any of my laid out plans for how this was going to go down because I know all those plans could easily go out the window, however I did really want to have a home

IM NOT AFRAID.

I WAS
BORN
TO DO THIS.

– JOAN OF ARC

I am grateful for the time I took away to find myself and create my own life. It allowed me the space to forgive and to love again, in a way I never had before.

birth. That was the most important thing to me. I loved the idea of my baby being born in the place where he or she would grow up.

That and I did not want to know the sex of the baby. There aren't very many surprises in life and this was one where I had a choice. I decided not to know and Bill agreed to 'not know' with me. I was convinced it was a girl and Bill was convinced it was a boy so we both picked out a first name for what we thought it was. We didn't know what to do with the last name since we weren't married. We agreed if it was going to be a girl she would carry my last name and if it was to be a boy, it would be Bill's. Looking back, I was surprised how accepting Bill was of this idea.

So fairly late into the pregnancy, the baby didn't seem to be moving in the direction of coming out any time soon, we held off as long as we could until there came a time where we had to begin inducing the pregnancy. The hospital, growing concerned now that I was two weeks and two days over the due date, gave me a choice of either continuing to try to naturally induce him on my own and having to end up coming into the hospital likely on a day where the doctor on duty would force a C-Section, or go in to the hospital now and work with a doctor who would allow natural birth providing I was safe in the process. I jumped at the chance to avoid the C-Section doctor, and decided to head in to be induced.

The birthing process wasn't fun. I don't think I'm alone in saying that however, I was now facing birth with doctors I had never met before as I had only worked with midwives until this point. One in particular strongly encouraging a C-Section as if that was the only option when he knew I wanted anything but. Something inside me knew it didn't have to be that way. And another doctor questioning my weight-gain during the pregnancy while another decides to inform me then that my baby would likely be born with Down Syndrome (because of a small nucal fold of skin at the back of his neck, already predetermined as 'normal' by the genetics testing we had gone through early on in the pregnancy). I was convinced the genetics testing was a waste of time as I was having this baby no matter what but it was encouraged to be aware of any challenges we may face.

You can imagine my frustration at this point, in what was supposed to be a memorable, once in a life-time experience.

Bill lost it and had to leave the room, I was arguing with the doctor about my weight and my my baby's genetics testing. It was chaos! All of sudden out of nowhere, a bold nurse named Sandra, marched into the room like a superhero, picked up the chart, looked me in the eyes, glanced at the doctors and announced 'We're having a natural birth today, I've decided to pick you, Emma, this is going to happen!" Amy, my Doula (there to help me through the contractions) and I looked at each other and thought 'Thank God!'

The induction itself took forever! What was supposed to be 8-10mg of Petocin (to induce contractions) took over 26 mg before I even began to feel anything. My baby was in no rush. The doctors repeatedly checked in on me asking if I was ok. I would enthusiastically respond with total poise, "I'm GREAT thank you!" just to make sure they left the room and left me alone. Finally, hours and hours later, as I sat on a large blue exercise ball that Bill had just carried through the entire hospital from the car- it was on. It hit me. I was about to give birth. For real, the pretending was over.

Amy, my Doula begain meditating with me to keep me focused. She kept saying "ride the wave" and at first I giggled. I actually almost burst out laughing. But I knew she knew what she was doing. So I just listened. She would talk me through the wave coming in and going out and then eventually I was in a deep meditative state. I remember thinking 'wow this is amazing, I am totally rocking this'. So much so, that I remember squatting in the shower in the middle of the contractions thinking 'Bill has been standing over me for a while, he really should grab a seat and sit down. "Bill, you should really have a seat. Can somebody get Bill a chair, please!!!."

At one point, I knew if this didn't hurry up, I was going to end up in a C-Section. The aesthetician was hovering around me, hoping to have a job to do, making me nervous so I told him to "Fuck off!" a little more stern than I even expected to come out my mouth. He went sulking out of the room and in comes the first doctor as if to give me one last chance. He looked me in the eyes as I held myself up on the edge of the bed to face him directly and he asked "How much energy do you have left, Emma?". I was done. But I knew if I uttered those words, the aesthetician would be right back in here and I'd have lost the battle of the doctors vs the midwives. Emma vs the knife. I couldn't let that happen. I pulled every ounce of energy together, perked up and vibrantly announced "I have SO much energy! I feel amazing!". This was a total bold-faced lie.

As if I had asked for it, at that very moment, in came the midwives! Saved! They immediately had me push in a different way, allowing my hips to really open up, and not even five minutes later, I thought I screamed in agony on the final push- only to find out after that at most, I let out a wimpy little moan 'erhhhhhh'. My baby was born. Desperately awaiting to hear the sex of my baby, Bill yells over to me, 'It's a boy!' not really sounding surprised at the revealing of the sex.

Turns out, Bill had known the sex all along. Apparently at the genetic testing, Bill had seen he sex. He never told me, kept it a secret the entire time. Mind you, he didn't do a very good job and had I been paying attention I probably could have figured it out. He left telling me he knew it was a boy along, it was weird that he was completely ok with allowing the last name of the baby if it was girl, to be Smallbone instead of carrying his name. And the girl name I had picked out was totally airy-fairy, he never called me on it. It was obvious he knew all along, come to think of it.

This medium missed that one.

After my son was born, I knew I needed to do something. I knew I needed to invite my dad back into my life. It had been seven years, in which I had found my voice, my life and myself. And somewhere in there I had forgiven him. I had forgiven him through healing and accepting myself.

I wanted my son to have his grandparents in his life. And I was finally in a place where I didn't think that had to be at expense of my self-confidence. At first I had a lot of rules for my parents, I needed to feel like I still had control of the situation but as time went on we grew closer and closer and we built the relationship we never had when I was growing up. I realize now, with my own child, there is no manual on how to raise one. We are all doing the best we can with what we know.

I am grateful for the time I took away to find myself and create my own life. It allowed me the space to forgive and to love again, in a way I never had before.

▼   ▼   ▼

U just smile and know it was meant to be.

EMMA'S EXERCISE • 6

▽

IDENTIFY SOME THEMES IN YOUR LIFE.
EXPLORE THEM AS IDEAS.

Timing is everything, and mostly out of your control. But what is in your control, is your awareness of opportunity and possibility.

Sometimes in life we think we know where we are going, therefore we put our blinders up to everything else. It's amazing what awareness can bring into our lives if we let it. Just like there were themes for me that I couldn't ignore, you have the same- we all do. These themes lead to the lessons that we need to learn, the lessons that will keep showing up as long as we ignore them. So build your awareness around the themes in your life and watch the doorways open up.

Write down some recurring themes in your life. Explore all areas such as relationships, work, passions, money, things you are good at.

Pick one of the themes that you aren't particularly focused on right now and ask these questions...

- why are you choosing to ignore it?

- what would happen if you explored it?

- what is the worst case scenario if you go for it/get help/ figure it out?

- what will or won't happen if you don't?

We are wonderfully creative beings, the only species on the planet that has the critical thinking mental faculty. Use it. Explore, ask yourself tough questions and acknowledge the new awareness. When the time is right, if you are open to it, the opportunity will arise. Just like me and Bill.

NOTES:

_____

_____

_____

_____

_____

_____

_____

_____

_____

_____

_____

_____

_____

• TIMING IS EVERYTHING •

EVERYONE IS WAITING FOR THE
BIG SHINY
RAINBOW
LEADING TO THE
POT OF GOLD
WITH A UNICORN BESIDE IT
HOLDING A PLATE OF CUPCAKES SAYING

HERE'S
YOUR
SIGN!

STOP WAITING FOR THE BIG SIGN, IT'S NOT COMING.

Often in readings I am compelled to remind people that the lessons we are to learn are in the smallest things. Which is why we often miss them. So many of us are going day by day, week by week, year by year waiting for a big sign saying 'right this way please!'. You'll probably be waiting a while. It may happen, you may experience a significant emotional event that in retrospect created a turning point in your life, however you can learn much more efficiently by finding the small signs in your day to day life. They are there I promise. I know because I used to ignore them also. Today, I live by them.

One of the themes that had always shown up for me in my life was Spirit. Usually when I needed a bit of a course-correct, or when I needed to serve them or deliver some sort of message to others, sometimes even when I needed to receive a message myself. Before my son came along, my connection had started to gain strength. I was seeing Spirit more often- they were waking me up at all hours of the night. I was living in my element surrounded by nature and trees, and for the first time in my life I was truly happy and in love with me. With Spirit showing up more, I learned on a few occasions that I needed to develop my connection as a skill. One night in particular, I received a reminder that unless I developed some boundaries (and quick) I'd be awake all hours of the night managing the open portal of Spirit needing my help.

Bill and I were living in a new development area, along a road that was often called a cow path, barely lit yet it had become a bustling thoroughfare for traffic. Accidents were occurring on the regular, unfortunately resulting in many fatalities.

As mediums, we are somewhat of a beacon for those who have died-they seek us out knowing we can connect with them, especially if they don't know where they are.

As accidents would occur on this street and someone would die, sure enough they'd show up at my house, all hours of the night. For a while I just acknowledged them and moved on with my day or night, but every once in awhile I could sense they needed something. On this one particular occasion, I didn't have to sense whether or not they needed something, this was made perfectly clear to me. There had been an accident where a Mother and her young daughter had died. I didn't know there had been an accident at the time, I was lying in bed late at night just minding my own business when suddenly, two white faces came darting at me through the darkness in my bedroom. The woman was holding up her daughter close to my face, clearly distraught desperately wanting my attention she said "You need to tell her she's dead!" It was obvious to me at this point that the mother was disoriented, she didn't know she was dead too. She was trying to help her daughter cross over without realizing she too was in Spirit.

Calmly, I looked the mother in the eyes and responded with "YOU are dead". In an instant, it was like her energy just disappeared. Poof. Gone. As quickly as she came flying in. It was the first time I really ever communicated to Spirit in the way of a command. I had chit chatted before such as with the young boy when I was back in England, but never had I said something that had an impact like I did that night. I didn't really know for sure what had happened, but I assumed I had helped her cross over. Hopefully, or she would probably be back.

A few days later, the woman came back to visit, in a different form than she had appeared to me earlier that week. I was downstairs in our large living room called 'the big room', she appeared standing in the window with two big beautiful wings behind her, an angel. She just looked at me lovingly and said "thank you" then left.

This was the moment of knowing. A moment of complete clarity that what I had done, had helped her cross over. This was what I was meant to do.

It had always seemed incredibly normal to me to have Spirit around all the time, I just didn't see it as something I was supposed to

Stop waiting
for the
Big
sign

It's not
coming!

This was a moment... I had helped her cross over. This was what I was meant to do.

do. I just thought they were hanging around. I wasn't paying attention. I wasn't listening to my gut. And I was completely missing the lessons, the signs along the way. I decided that I was going to start paying attention, I was going to start listening to learning what I could do to help. But after my son was born I suffered from postpartum depression. I had incredibly low energy, I struggled to get the sleep I needed and just felt drained. Having suffered from depression and anxiety at different times in my life, and a few major breakdowns, this uneasiness was familiar to me. Yet this time was different. I recognized how I was feeling and that I needed to do something, that in fact I was the only one who could do something. I just wasn't sure what.

I went to visit my good friend Cheri who often had some wisdom for me when I couldn't see it see it myself. As we sat on her front porch together having a cup of tea I could tell she worried about me. I was worried about me too. Cheri asked me a few questions about why I was feeling negative, what might change how I was feeling and what was it that I felt I needed to do. There was really only one thing in my life that was still left undone. Undiscovered. That was my mediumship. It was the theme that kept showing up for me in small ways, and apart from a few standout experiences, I really hadn't explored its purpose or tried to understand how it could fit into my life, how I might be able to help people with it. We made a couple of phone calls together and found a local Spiritualist church that had a class coming up the following weekend. Finally, I had something to look forward to even if I had no idea what to expect. This would also be my first visit to a church, other than to sight-see a historical landmark. I wasn't even sure they'd let us in.

Off we went the following weekend, to meet the facilitator and explore The Spiritualist Church of Galt. This church was unlike any other. It was a little unassuming white house with a wooden porch attached to the front. As we sat in a chair circle waiting patiently to begin the first class, Val, a medium from England (my home country!) calmly entered the room as the facilitator. I don't know if I was expecting a cape and a crystal ball but she was just as unassuming as the little white church I had walked into only minutes before.

As it turns out, this unassuming woman in the unassuming church, on this unassuming weekend changed my life. It's funny how it's often the unassuming things that do.

Val reminded me in a way, of my grandmother. She was sweet, funny and straight to the point. We connected instantly, I felt a real sense of calm around her. I was able to be completely open about how I had felt and what I had experienced in my life. It was wonderful. Val had asked me why I hadn't explored my mediumship until now, if I'd had access to it my whole life. I shared with her that I felt I had made a decision to stop communicating with Spirit until recently, that I had closed a door in college and I couldn't open it anymore. She scoffed at me and replied "Well then, bloody-well open it, my dear!" I never looked back.

I had started classes with Val in the summer when it was hot so I was always barefoot. I'm a barefoot girl most of the time anyway! But when it started to get cold and I had to put my shoes on, giving messages got harder for me. I asked Val, 'It seems like I need to be barefoot?' To which she responded "Then be barefoot!" It was like I was finally given permission to be myself. It was almost like my control mechanism. I could let Spirit know I was ready when I took my shoes off. This didn't stop them from showing up when I had my shoes on, mind you, just limited the stream of consciousness somewhat.

I knew I was different, even in a room full of mediums.

I started attending the little white church regularly, taking the classes for mediumship. I was having fun learning and found it a welcome distraction from the postpartum depression. But something happened as I began exploring this side of me. I realized I had a real gift, I was good at it. So good, that one night after a few of the classes, I was asked to stand up at the church and give messages. Every Wednesday night the church hosts an open invitation evening where mediums stand up and share messages with the guests from their loved ones who had passed.

I loved these evenings so much and felt honoured to be able to stand up with the other mediums and share my gift. I could see how it was helping people for the first time. I had found my home. It felt so right.

I never questioned my mediumship, but at one time I did question the purpose of it and my ability to find my groove with it. Deep down I knew I would eventually, what I didn't know is that it would take the right environment to flip the confidence switch to 'ON'.

The first message I ever gave was on a Wednesday evening. I took off my shoes as I headed up to the front of the crowd, barefoot. It became my thing. The audience was eagerly awaiting their message, as was I. I wasn't nervous, I was excited to give the gift I had watched other mediums give. I was in my element, it felt so natural to stand up and deliver what was being communicated to me, through me.

The Spirit made me dance. It was like I could feel the castanets in my hands, I wanted to stomp my foot and dance around the church.

One of the messages I received was from a woman who had taken care of a woman in the audience. She even described the playground she would take her to when she was young girl. I could tell this message had a big impact on her, I knew I had made a difference for her. After the evening finished, she came up to me to thank me again. She asked if she could come and see me for a one-on-one. "Yes!" I said, thinking I'll have to figure out what that would look like later. I had never even thought about having one-on-one sessions but it felt like the right next step. I'd done plenty of photography one on ones before- I guess that was my training ground for my mediumship clients. Same thing, sort of.

I went on to build my one-on-one client base fairly organically. Part of me didn't want my mediumship to become a business, part of me wanted to keep it all to myself, my happy place. So I gave myself a goal of 25 one-on-one sessions before I would take this seriously as a business. Well, those 25 sessions came and went in the blink of an eye. Before I knew it, I had a medium business with new clients, repeat clients and requests for group events all over the place. I was shocked at how easily all of this had come.

I gave messages at the church for some time before the church moved to a lovely new spot just outside Cambridge. It truly felt like home. The energy in this new home was magic. But not for long. Shortly after this move, I was told that the next time I stood up to give messages, my shoes would have to be on. They wouldn't tolerate bare feet in the church and would require me to abide by the rules if I wanted to continue to give messages there. I was beyond upset. I didn't understand how they could impose rules on how we gave messages.

I mean really, we are a bunch of 'woo woo' people standing up giving messages from Spirit. I think it would be half expected that we be a little unique.

The church stood it's ground. And I knew in that moment that I was supposed to stop giving messages there. Spirit had given me this gift of communication and they had made it clear that the barefoot thing was a necessity. So I had to go. I was heart-broken but I carried on with my one-on-ones and group sessions outside of the church. I started to love my group sessions and getting to know some regular clients. I wasn't just a medium for them, I was a guide, a confidant and a friend. But something was missing. I so badly wanted to take part in the church. I wanted to stand up with the other mediums and give messages. And I wanted to do it my way, barefoot. This was so important to me.

After I had been away from the church for a while, I went in one day to have a quick visit with Val after a flower reading. I needed to ask her what she thought, it was important to me. She thought it was silly that I wasn't able to give messages and asked me if I was still doing 'my thing' outside the church. I said of course. Her response was "Good Girl!" And for some reason that was all I needed to hear. I didn't need to be validated by the church- I was giving messages to people that needed them. It didn't matter where that was, just as long as I was using the gift I was born with.

A week or so after that conversation, Val had stood up one Sunday to give messages at the church. She knew I wasn't there. And she knew I hadn't been standing up giving messages and she knew I needed to. She spoke to the audience about mediumship. How it works, how it comes in all shapes and sizes for different kinds of people all over the world. Val talked about how there are no rules, if a medium wanted to give messages barefoot, this would need to be accepted in the eyes of the church and everyone there. I didn't know this had taken place until a friend had messaged me later in the evening to let me know that Val had shared her belief that what we wear and what we do shouldn't matter. All that matters is giving proof of life after death. She was reinforcing what Spiritualism stood for, reminding the church why we were here and helping me and my bare-feet-mediumship become accepted, as it should have been all along. I couldn't wipe the big cheesy grin off my face.

I now know, it had to go the way it did. I had to leave the church and build my confidence through one-on-one sessions, build my community, find my own way. Here I am now, completely confident in the church as a medium, ready more than ever to stand up and share my gift. Had I continued giving messages at the church I may never have ventured out to build my own brand and business. It was the sign that I was meant for greater things, and I was finally listening.

I honestly think it was Spirit preventing me from being here, to help me grow myself as a medium in order to come back stronger.

I started to develop my own style of giving messages because I had the confidence to do so. I was different. I always made an effort to include absolutely everyone in the room. For every message I gave, I shared a personal story and a teaching point so the entire audience could take something away. I believe everyone in the room needs to feel included as they could each benefit or learn form someone else's message. After all, they are there for a reason. This is what truly set me apart. And the reason I have the loyal community and client base I do today.

Each little decision was a stepping stone to the life I lead today. Small signs that at the time didn't make sense but in retrospect cannot be discounted for the way in which they guided me.

EMMA'S EXERCISE • 7

▽

STOP LOOKING FOR THE BIG SIGNS.
PAY ATTENTION TO EVERYTHING.

First of all, you need to trust your gut. If you think it is a sign- it is. Spirit needs us to trust them and ourselves. They are not going to throw a billboard in your face that says "THIS IS A SIGN!" Unless you choose to see the little signs as big billboards. It's all in your perspective.

I think the relationship we foster with Spirit is built on trust. You, trusting yourself and you, trusting Spirit. It's a sort of faith that we are connected, a belief beyond what we can see. I think that's what people truly come to see me for.

Everyone's signs are different. Everyone's gut feeling will be different. You have to tune into what feels right for you. What are your signs? Explore all the little things, see them as signs and notice how often they show up for you.

Start a 'weird shit journal'. Make a list of the odd things you see on the regular.

Are they numbers? An object or symbol? Is it a sound, or something in nature? Or a tingle down your right arm like me?

I see ravens and crows by the dozens, everyday. Without fail. And they just happen to be a symbol of the connection to Spirit and the afterlife. They are also a reminder of the magic around us.

Once you start to notice and trust your signs, Spirit will show you more.

I HAVE CHOSEN TO BE

HAPPY

BECAUSE IT IS FOR
THE GOOD
OF MY HEALTH.

- VOLTAIRE

CHOOSE HAPPINESS.

▼ 8

It's a different kind of life that I'm living, I know. It is one that is still largely questioned, although much more accepted than even ten years ago. I see the world opening up to the idea that there is more than this physical world we know and love, there has to be.

In my newfound purposeful life, I still meet with skeptics and people who don't want to believe that I could have access to something they don't understand. Even amongst family. But what has changed is my need to fit in and be accepted. It's gone. I spent my whole life trying to fit someone else's mould, only to find that I am happiest when I'm my true self, unapologetically.

I knew this was what I was meant to do the day I did a reading for my dad. The man whom I felt never good enough for- was finally proud of me. I could feel it. I can't help but think it was because I was finally proud of me and he could feel it.

It was the first and only time I did a reading for him, he hadn't asked until he heard a message for my mum and knew it was something I couldn't have possibly known. We were sitting inside his house in the snug just off the kitchen, as I began to connect, and suddenly my son woke up. So I suggested we take a walk outside and head to the backyard where my dad had created a beautiful garden there was a patio and a big veggie garden and a patch of grass. As we were walking his beloved sister showed up. She walked with us outside towards the garden, all the while chatting with us saying "Isn't this nice Freddy! You've done such a good job on the garden!". When I shared this with my dad, he looked at me in shock. His sister had always called him 'Freddy' when she was alive, this I could not have known. As we sat down in the garden shed (what we call the cottage), his father showed up. I began describing my grandfather in detail to my dad, things that my dad didn't even know. I could see that he walked with a limp, his left ankle was busted and so he would tie his boot really tight- he just lived with it that way to avoid going to a doctor. My dad didn't remember this so he later phoned his older sister, my Aunt Diana, she confirmed his left ankle was broken and he refused to see a doctor to have it fixed.

I told my dad that I could see his dad leaning over an old wooden box that he had set up as a workstation, where he fixed things; electronics, televisions and small engines. My dad just looked at me amazed and said "Yep". I could see the tears welling in his eyes with recollection. I had never felt pride from my dad the way I did at this moment. His dad let me know that he wanted to hold my dad's hand and apologize for his shortcomings as a father. My dad choked up. It was an apology he thought he would never get.

I know my dad was proud of my photography work, he just always pushed me to be doing more like it was never enough. This was the day where I felt like I was enough, just as I am. It's similar to what I see in Bill. I see his pride in my work as a medium, the impact it has on my clients, myself and as a result- my family.

For a long time, I waited to hear the words, 'I'm proud of you, Emma.' They never came. But I've realized, they didn't have to. I could feel it in my dad's presence, and I still do today. Up until the day he died, my father had many questions for me about how it all worked and what it felt like to be a medium- he wanted to know everything. I believe we set his GPS before he left this physical world, which made it easier for him to transition and easier for us to communicate now. Which we do often.

Shit happens. Alot. To everyone. In life, every day, every moment is a chance to choose happiness.

To look back on my life up until now, it was obvious all along what I was meant to be doing. But I wouldn't be who I am today had I not experienced what I did.

And as hard as it may feel sometimes, it is a choice. How do you choose to feel happy, you might ask? By choosing what you focus on. I know we all have shit. Trust me, I've had my fair share. So what

EXPERIENCE
IS THE
GREATEST
TEACHER.

separates the happy people from the sad people? The happy people have problems too, it's just how they look at them and what they choose to focus their attention to.

You have to make a conscious decision to see the good. And sometimes to peel back some layers to find the good. In every experience there is an opportunity to learn something. Some of our greatest learnings come from our most challenging experiences. Why? Because we don't really learn other wise. We are creatures of habit and sometimes we have to be hit over the head a few times with a baseball bat to get it. Instead of blaming the bat, thank the bat- for there could have been a sledgehammer waiting behind the bat just in case you didn't get the message.

My dad, for all the challenges I experienced with him, was probably my greatest teacher. In my relationship with him I learned acceptance, forgiveness, unconditional love and how to communicate amongst many other things. The strength I have today is because of him. My drive, my commitment to my work, my want for the best, I owe to him. And for that, I am grateful.

EMMA'S EXERCISE • 8

▽

GRATITUDE IS YOUR GATEWAY TO SPIRIT.

One of the most magical of practises, referred to as gratitude can change your entire perspective on life. Gratitude or the act of feeling grateful for anything expands us in ways we didn't think possible and connects us to Spirit, universal energy. When we truly feel thankful, appreciative and full of love for what we have, who we are and the life inside of us we can find the beauty in everything, even the tough stuff we experience in life.

What I love sharing with people is that Spirit is trying to give us signs and gifts every day in order to move forward. When you can feel grateful for the guidance, you'll build a stronger connection to it. Every time I identify a sign or a message, or take a moment and say out loud, 'THANK YOU!' And every single time I do, I build a bond with my sense of knowing, the trust grows and I cement my belief in my ability to connect with Spirit.

So start small. Set a goal for 90 days to wake up every morning and write what you are grateful for in a daily journal. If you would like to pay it forward then post it online on your social media to inspire others to do the same. Start with the obvious and you'll see each day you'll find more and more wonderful things in your life to feel grateful for.

Here are some ideas you can start with...

I am grateful that I am alive to take on the day!

I am grateful for the ability to see the beautiful world and all it's vibrant colour!

I am grateful for the abundance the universe gives me!

I am grateful for the food in my fridge and the coffee in my cupboard!

You get the point. Starting your day on a positive note shifts your energy. It gives you the awareness of your surroundings and it makes you take notice of and feel grateful for the small things in life. Gratitude is where you can start to truly connect with and let Spirit in.

What are you grateful for?

NOTES:

_____

_____

_____

_____

_____

_____

_____

_____

_____

_____

COMMUNICATION IS THE ESSENCE OF HUMAN LIFE

- J LIGHT

COMMUNICATION IS EVERYTHING, ESPECIALLY WITH YOURSELF.

Communication is truly everything. What to know how well you communicate with people? Take a look at your relationships. Want to know how you communicate with yourself? Pay attention to how you feel.

Why do we struggle to communicate so much? Why do we struggle to express what we are thinking and how we feel? Why do we have such a hard time truly listening to others and understanding them, where they are at and where they're coming from?

I think it's a bit of fear, a bit of adopted habit, some early experiences that have us clam up to avoid any further pain in life. A concoction of reasons why we just block it all. We block communication coming in, we block communication going out and we are even clever enough to block it inside ourselves too. Block, block, block-ity block. It's just safer that way. Right? Wrong! Safer for who? Not you. You'll bubble up in big ball of unexpressed emotion, stress, and anger- inevitable to explode at some point, probably on an unsuspecting victim who just happened to be around at the time you hit the breaking point. And anything you are supposed to be listening to or understanding can't find it's way in because you are so full of your own unexpressed shit. This is honestly how most of us live, we just don't know any better.

How do we fix it? Communicate! Take the shit helmet off and communicate how you feel!!!

Say what you need to say. Express yourself, learn how to do it in a way that it reaches the other person positively, and receive it in a way that they feel understood. Isn't the truth supposed to set us free?

If you can't say it out loud without scaring yourself, you probably shouldn't say it silently to yourself either.

If you want to learn to communicate with the outside world, you must learn to communicate with the inside world. Start with how you talk to yourself.

I believe that we are all here on Earth to figure out one thing. And for each of us that one thing is different. I've learned that my one thing is communication. There have been times in my life where I have completely sucked at it. Many examples of which you have read about in this book such as not talking to my dad about how he made me feel for the first 32 years of my life. The friends I grew up with, E. The list goes on.

In retrospect, each of the major challenges I have faced in my life are connected to one common theme. Communication. With myself, with my family and with Spirit. And the reason I would lack communication on any of these occasions wasn't because I couldn't communicate or engage in an open, honest discussion about what I needed or wanted, but because I chose not to.

▶   **Communication with myself.**   ◀

My entire life I have had a complicated internal dialogue. I think we all do to some extent and part of life is learning to listen to it, change it and eventually create it.

I was three years old when Spirit showed up so I've had company for most of my life. It was a strange place to be as a kid. Alone in a social sense, yet surrounded by Spirit from another world. Why were they drawn to me if real people weren't? Why did I see them and no one else did? I still don't know why but I've learned to see the magic in not knowing. Maybe there are some things we aren't meant to know or understand. Either way, my relationship to Spirit always reflected my relationship with myself. Letting Spirit in had to mean letting go of the need to fit in with everyone else. And that scared me. My biggest problem was that I wasn't communicating with myself. Some of the things I said to myself, I wouldn't dare say out loud- which was probably a good sign that I shouldn't have been saying it at all.

I was too busy listening to everyone else. I grew up listening to the Spirit world, the nasty kids at school, my teachers, my family and all the people who were never ready to accept me the way that I was. I began to talk to myself the same way, I didn't know any better. I just thought majority rules. They were probably all right and I'd better hurry up and try and be normal or I'd get left behind. My self-talk became hurtful, angry and full of hate. I was too busy searching for understanding outside of myself, I didn't realize how much I was hurting my self-esteem in the process.

Be careful with what you say to yourself. You are listening. And you need only to hear words of encouragement, strength and love. With that, you can do anything.

▶ **Communication with my family.** ◀

As I grew older, my fathers voice played a major role in my internal dialogue. I heard his voice before I heard my own. It took me 32 years to make a decision to take my voice back. And that took courage and commitment.

I struggled at school outside of sports and my real interest subjects like science and visual arts. I didn't fit in or have any real friends. The other kids teased and poked fun at me, calling me names and singling me out in front of the class. But my biggest challenge wasn't at school- I could handle all of that for the most part. My biggest challenge was at home. My dad and I never saw eye to eye, and I can honestly say I hated him for most of my life. Today, it's a horrible thought, but one I grew so comfortable with for so long, I almost forgot why I felt that way until he gave me another reason to perpetuate the hurt later in life.

I'm not sure where it started, but I can pinpoint a time in my life where I was searching for my own identity. I saw my reflection in my dad, and it scared me.

My dad was tough on me growing up. I'm sure he saw me fading in and out of depression. I know now, he was doing the best he could, while watching his only daughter slowly shy away from the world into the shadows of her former, boisterous, adventurous self. But at the time, I resented him for interfering. He became controlling, dominant and derogatory. I felt as thought I couldn't do anything right. Nothing was ever good enough for him and I tried hard to meet his expectations for many years. I felt like I was failing him, faltering at every move. I didn't have a head for numbers, I struggled to get math right, I worked out in a gym to the point of insanity. I worked a job to earn money but it was never enough. I could feel it.

I needed space. I needed to listen to my own emotions, create my own thoughts and my own environment. Most of my life, I had been living with everyone else's.

I wanted my dad's acceptance, I craved it. I wanted to be liked at school, I was desperate for it. But the truth was I didn't like or accept myself. I had been too busy looking for their approval, I didn't even know what it looked like to have my own. It took me a long time to realize, that this silence is my sanctuary. My place to find the courage I needed to move forward.

When I did, I also found the courage to say what I needed to say. For so long I lived in fear of what my dad thought of me, I'd never had the courage to say what I thought of me. I needed to hear the words come out of his mouth "I am proud of you, Emma" but I was unwilling to give them to myself. When I made the decision to make words count, to him and everyone else, to stand up for myself and let people know when they hurt me… I changed my life. I found the power to create the world around me, instead of be a participant in it.

Creating your world takes courage, most often with the people closest to you.

▶   **Communication with Spirit.**   ◀

Spirit is all around us ever-present. To choose to communicate with Spirit is to knowingly be present, acknowledge the magic around us and feel grateful for all that we are. That is it in its most simplest form. As that connection grows stronger, so will your signals of Spirit's existence.

I weaved in and out of my connection with Spirit, taking the gift I have for granted for many years. There came a point where I questioned my own sanity, if no one else could see it then was it possible I was making it all up? For a while in the shit helmet I couldn't 'see' Spirit so I began to believe it was all a figment of my imagination. Over the years it would show up every now and then, fleetingly. Sometimes they wanted something, other times it was just a ghostly figure sitting with me as I watched tv, unobtrusive, just letting me know they were there. I'd get shivers and goosebumps and hear people's voices. But I didn't trust it like I did when I was a kid. Until I found a confidence within myself. Until I explored it's purpose in my life and practised feeling a connection with it. It took healing and time, and a knowing.

'I am not what happened to me, I am what I choose to become.'
—CG Jung

I work often with people who have unresolved issues, such as I would have had if I had not let my father back into my life after my son came along. I am entirely grateful to the relationship we developed later in life, the lost time we made up for and the peace and love I feel towards him today. A part of what I teach every time I speak, is that our conversations are what make our relationships. We are what we say, and to avoid stepping over some boundaries or limits sometimes we may never truly express ourselves, or resolve our issues with one another. This can be damaging. Condemning our souls to exist in unrest, until we make peace with the unsaid.

And so, I urge you. Say what you need to say. Apologize, Forgive and find the good in every opportunity to choose a label. Find peace now. Otherwise you'll be looking for me on the other side to help you.

EMMA'S EXERCISE • 9

HONESTY IS THE BEST POLICY.
WHAT DO YOU REALLY WANT?

Communication with yourself is the most important thing you can do to create peace and abundance in your own life.

Let's start with what is most important to your own Spiritual growth. What are your wants, needs and desires? Do you know? It is in this exploration of desire you will find some hidden meaning, some idea of your purpose and where you should focus in life. But before you do this exercise, I want you to promise yourself that you will be completely honest with yourself.

- Make a list of the top three things you want to achieve in your life. Big scary goals!

- Ask yourself the following questions and be brutally honest with yourself here.

  - Are they your Partner's/Father/Mother/Children's wants, needs or desires?

  - Are they what society thinks you should do, the 'norm' for people in today's economy?

  - Are they what you've already started in life, so it's easier just to continue?

  - Are they limited what you think you can achieve instead of what you really want?

- Now, after reflecting on these goals, write the list again but this time consider the following...

  - If there were no limitations of money/time/effort or societal/family pressure, what would those three things be?

- Lastly, explore why these are important to you. WHY do you want to achieve these goals?

Communication with yourself is the most important thing you can do to create peace and abundance in your own life.

Now you're starting to let Spirit in!

NOTES:

_____

_____

_____

_____

_____

_____

_____

_____

_____

_____

• COMMUNICATION IS EVERYTHING •

WHAT IF IT IS JUST THE BEGINNING?

WHAT IF DEATH ISN'T THE END?

Death isn't final at all. It feels final, because we don't have much understanding of the Spirit world, where we go after death, or even where we came from. If you take nothing else from this book, this is what I want you to get. Our loved ones, our ancestors are here, every minute, ever-present, in all places. You can talk to them. You may not hear them like I do, you may not see them like I do but this is a mere inconvenience to the truth. They hear you.

This past year, has been an extraordinary one in so many ways. Most extraordinary for me, was experiencing the very gift I share with so many others, personally. Don't get me wrong, every time I share a message with you I am experiencing it just as much as you are, if not more as an empath, however this time for the first time, I was on the receiving end of a message from my own Dad.

There is nothing in this life more shocking than death. Even anticipated death.

We had known my father was ill for about a year, we watched as he deteriorated, eventually struggling to do the things that we take for granted such as drawing in the very oxygen we need to live. I had come to appreciate my dad in many ways, ways that in the seven silent years we had, I could never have imagined the peace and acceptance we share today. My mother and I didn't really believe he could leave us, although if attached to a polygraph we'd have been forced to admit his death was imminent. While I have spent years counselling others through the loss of loved ones, it almost seemed impossible that I could lose someone I loved. I was here to help others, I didn't want to have to help myself through the same thing.

I was in on a regular schedule of readings and events now, in full swing of my mediumship, wife-ship and motherhood, thoroughly enjoying the journey of exploration I was on.

I wasn't ready for my new found life to be disrupted yet. I wonder if we ever are.

It was July of 2014 when the news came that my dad had been diagnosed with Idiopathic Pulmonary Fibrosis which is a hardening of the lungs, ultimately a death sentence in a relatively short period of time. Exactly how long, we didn't know. With Idiopathic Pulmonary Fibrosis, the lungs turn to rock, they become a solid mass making it very difficult to breathe. It's like drowning. It was assumed, however, that he would survive with a lung transplant. We knew we were in for a bumpy ride but we remained hopeful and convinced this was just a hiccup, as he had always been extremely healthy. We thought he was invincible.

We think he had been living with the disease for 10-15 years already. An accumulation of his work in a machine factory breathing in metal, riding sidecar breathing in dirt and to top it off, he grew up down the street from a rubber factory. Each on it's own a potential factor in the diagnosis, the combination of all three, I am sure, were definitive contributors to the disease. But the 'Idiopathic' part means we will never really know the cause. We were shocked that this seemingly healthy, vibrant man could be facing such an illness, deterioration of the very organ from which he breathes.

He had started to decline severely in September, just a few months after the diagnosis we watched his health spiral very quickly from that point on. And not even six months later in February of 2015, my mother was no longer able to bathe him on her own. She lived in constant fear of a fall he might not recover from without readily available medical support. Finally, we brought him to hospital in hopes the disease had done enough damage to get him on the transplant list, for which he had to be really sick, but not sick enough that any of his other organs had been compromised.

What if death isn't the end. What if it is just the beginning?

Once in hospital, my brother, my mother and I all thought we were just one step closer to that life-saving transplant. It was just a matter of time now, and we would be going home with him and his new set of lungs! It was just less than a week before mine and my brother's birthday and Bill and I had a few days booked at St. Anne's Spa in Coburg. My mum encouraged us to still go and she would let us know if we needed to return. Before we left on the 4 hour road trip east, I went to visit my dad.

He was barely able to speak now so I took with me a video of my son singing a song. All he did was play it over and over and over again. When it was time to leave, I gave him a big huge hug, kissed him on the head twice and told him I loved him 3 or 4 times. Walking out that day, I felt so grateful that I had given him all my energy in that moment. I made sure he really knew that I loved him.

That night after a day of spa-ing, Bill and I were about to retire for the night when my mum called around 11:30pm. She let me know he wasn't looking good, but to stay the night and come home in the morning. My gut told me in that moment, I had to go. We decided to leave immediately and checked out at midnight, St Anne's did everything they could to accommodate, going above and beyond for us. Shortly after midnight we began the long drive back home to Cambridge, then on to London where dad was in hospital. It was the shittiest drive imaginable, one of the craziest storms I have seen, I'm not even sure how Bill drove through it- I could barely see.

During the drive I was meditating, thinking of my dad sending healing energy. I had learned in Reiki that you can hold the image of someone in your mind and heal them, from a distance. At one point I stopped to look at my watch. It was 1:39 am and I heard my dad's voice as if he was in the back seat "Hey Em". I shot up in the passenger seat and said "What the fuck!" I knew I had to do something, I knew that meant he had left his body so I yelled at him, "You get back in your fucking body and you stay there until I can get there, and Mum can get there! And Grandma? Aunt

Helen? You need to make sure he stays there until I get there!".
The next instant, he was gone.

When we got to the hospital the next day, I told my mum that
Dad had come to me in the car, I'd hear 'Hey Em' around 1:39am
and told him to get back into his body until I got home, then
he was gone. She confirmed that that would have been around
the time he had suffered a heart failure and died, briefly, before
the doctors and nurses revived him (going against procedure
by over-administering drugs to do so). As a result they had put
him into an induced coma to preserve his state and prevent any
further trauma.

Over the next few days I began to do Reiki on him. At first I could
feel him take the energy from me, almost like it was being pulled
from my hands. The numbers on the machines would stabilize
briefly and his heart rate would come down. As the days went on
I could feel the effects of Reiki weakening. It was like that energy
was being sucked from me but it was going nowhere. It was
then that I knew he wasn't here anymore. I knew at that moment
he had left his body. I went and joined my mum in the lounge,
looked in her eyes as I sat down and said "Mum, you know he's
not there anymore right?' She said 'Yes, I know'.

*I don't think we control when someone passes, yet I believe we
were given the gift of time in my father's passing. We needed
those few days to make sense of it all. Those few days felt like a
long time. Time in which we could come to terms with his death.*

On the Friday morning, the day before mine and Richard's birthday,
the doctor came to the room in which we were sitting with my
lifeless dad in the bed, all hooked up with tubes and machines
keeping his body alive. We knew a transplant was no longer
possible. With the heart failure his heart was now far too weak to
withstand a surgery of that kind. We had found out he had also
had pneumonia (we suspect he was keeping this from us for a
while) and his lungs were far more damaged than first anticipated.
We faced the ultimate decision to turn off the machines. Mum let
us know he didn't want to be revived if a transplant wasn't on the
table for him, he just wanted palliative care until he passed.

You must
experience
it all for
yourself

Your own
connection
to Spirit

Once we had made the decision and called in my brother just moments before he was to attend a job interview- during which we wouldn't have been able to reach him, I had a holy shit moment. The following day, when we were organizing to switch off the machines, was my birthday. Selfishly, I asked Mum if we could hold off for a day, to not have my father pass on my birthday. I felt so bad that I was asking for us to prolong his suffering so my birthday could remain death-free for the rest of my life, yet it turned out the organ transplant team who were to receive his organs as a donation could not arrive until the following day anyway. Phew! I was saved from the guilt.

The day we were to turn the machines off began the Smallbone way- we all arrived to his room high in energy, wishing the nursing staff 'Good morning!' to which they all nervously nodded and looked at each other concerned for us. My mum whispers to them 'We know', just in case it looked like we didn't. We were trying to be positive no matter what, even if that didn't look right to anyone else. The nursing staff were incredible, they allowed us to do what we needed to say goodbye. My mum just wanted to lay in bed with him to get as close as possible, they had been together their whole life. So the staff lowered the bed for her and took most of his tubes off the one side so she could get real close. I could only spend short amounts of time in there, I had to often take breaks as the energy in the place was overwhelming for me. I could feel all of it.

Finally the moment came, when our lives would be forever changed. The doctor talked us through what was going to happen as they turned off all the machines. It took almost half an hour for him to actually pass on. We were waiting for him to let go, wondering when it was going to happen. His dead mother and sister were waiting for him to cross over at the head of his bed as we watched on and waited. I was so busy being the daughter I had forgotten I may be able to help. Suddenly, I snapped out of it. 'Shit! Spirit, what do I do?'

Spirit told me to 'Take his hand and walk him over to where my Granny and Aunt Helen were. 'How do I do that?' I asked. They said 'help him, help him walk over'. So I closed my eyes and imagined myself holding his hand. I walked him to the back of the bed towards where his mum and his sister were waiting for him. It was a matter of seconds after that, my dad passed. It made sense to me that his mum and sister were the guide for him to cross over. He loved them very much.

There is so much in my life that I am grateful for. My dad's passing is one of them. Don't get me wrong I'd give anything to have him back, however I feel more connected to him today than I ever did in the physical form. I am grateful for the time we spent together after we reconnected, I am grateful for the time he spent with my son, being a part of his life. I am grateful for the connection we now have, with him in Spirit, I can truly say today that I love him with all my heart. And I feel it right back, I know he loves me too. But I didn't say goodbye the day he left his body. This is what I want you to understand. You don't need to say goodbye either, they are still here with you.

Even if you can't see what I see, you can feel them.

Having experienced myself, what I help others with everyday-loss, grief and the sadness that comes with a loved one's death, I feel you every time you walk through the door looking for answers. I know you're hurting. They know you're hurting. But you don't have to go through it alone.

So my question is... What if death isn't the end. What is if it is just the beginning?

Since the moment my dad has passed, I have been strongly guided on the path to Spirit.

Even how this book came about is a bit miraculous to me. All of the events leading up to this moment have been magic. I now know first hand that our loved ones in Spirit are trying to push us forward. They are trying to push us in the direction we are meant to go. Not the one we think we should go in, but the one we were born to go in, our purpose.

What if when we pass we can do more good for our loved ones

because we can truly see what they need? And we can actually help them get to their destination! I think life is just the training ground for our after life.

And this is why I tell you, that my words- this book aren't enough. You MUST experience it all for yourself, your own connection to Spirit. Take off the shit-helmet, listen to your gut and pay attention to the signs and the themes that show up in your life. It may not look the same for you as it did for me, but you too, can connect in your own way. Like anything, it takes practise.

This connection to Spirit is a part of all of us, it's how you acknowledge it and what you do with it that will make all the difference.

Really all I do now is take off my shoes and wait for a tingle down my right arm. It's my sign that Spirit has arrived. Once I connect with Spirit, they use that same tingle to let me know when I'm on the right track. That's my signal and you need to find yours. It may not be a tingle, it may not be your grandmother whispering 'cast a circle' or be obvious at all. There are messages in everything that is said to you, everything around you, everything that happens. It's not always going to be a mind-blowing punch in the face. It may simply be confirmation that you're in a good place, just keep moving forward.

Life is all about letting go and learning. Moving forward is more important than looking back.

You have an incredible ability to connect to Spirit and communicate the way I do. Most of us just have it switched to the 'off' position like I did for many years- afraid of it, unsure of it and in denial of it. So, in the wise words of Val, 'Turn the bloody thing back on!'

Start where you are, be grateful for what you have and look for the signs that you are surrounded by Spirit. They are there, I promise.

And if you're having trouble finding the connection, try taking your shoes off.

Works for me!

Love and light,

The Barefoot Medium

▼   ▼   ▼

EMMA'S EXERCISE • 10

▽

TALK TO YOUR LOVED ONES.
THEY ARE LISTENING.

People think they need to come to me to connect with Spirit. This couldn't be further from the truth. You come to me for validation. But your loved ones are always around you. You can speak to them whenever you like, and they'll hear you. You may not get a response back, at least in the way you want or the way I do, yet. Just know that they are listening.

Talk to them every day. Tell them what you want to say. Tell them how you are feeling and what you are thinking. Picture them with you, around you. Be with them, feel like they are beside you because truly, they aren't that far away.

Spend a little time each day talking to whom ever it is that you would like to engage with. It will feel funny at first, but you'll find a groove with it as the days go on, and maybe you'll even start to see some signs that they hear you!

- Picture your loved one with you having coffee in the morning, or by your side as you drive to work.

- Talk to them about how you feel, what you are thinking, or recount an experience you had with them that brings back fond memories.

- Notice how you feel and what's happening around you. Don't expect a sign back, just pay attention.

Fall in love with the idea that you can talk to them and you'll never think they aren't with you here. Which makes sense, because they never left you in the first place.

NOTES:

_____

_____

_____

_____

_____

_____

_____

_____

_____

_____

_____

_____

_____

_____

THE MEANING OF
LIFE
IS TO FIND YOUR
GIFT.
THE PURPOSE OF
LIFE
IS TO GIVE IT
AWAY.

- WILLIAM SHAKESPEARE

THE GIFT I GET TO GIVE.

▼

Up until now, you have heard my version of what I do and the impact it has had on me. However, I want to leave you with the thought that it's not about me. The purpose of this book is to build a relationship between you and the world that I know, your connection to Spirit and dear loved ones that have passed. I am simply the vessel for communication between you and your loved ones, Spirit, and a teacher of all of the principles I have shared with you thus far. Many of my clients have shared with me how their experience has changed their life, and so I have asked them to join me in this endeavour and share their experience with you.

The stories to follow are a small collection of some of the beautiful clients I have worked with over the past while. I hope you find some connection and joy in their stories and experiences, as much as I have enjoyed being a part of them.

Dear Amanda, Sara, Tara, Sarah and Melissa, I thank you from my heart for your contribution to this book- the beginning... of The Barefoot Medium.

▶   **Amanda's Story.**   ◀

Feeling self-conscious and totally awkward about bringing my baby to a local photographer meet-and-greet; I ran into Emma, full on body slam, with my baby girl fast asleep in a sling. "oh I'm so sorry, I've been cooped up for weeks and I just wanted to come and be around adults, let alone photographers" She just laughed and hugged me, we chatted about kids and photography and I totally dug her Spirit. We exchanged contact info and wanted to keep in touch, maybe go for coffee.

"I am a Medium and an Empath, I feel what Spirit feels and this helps me connect with them to share their messages for you."

Fast forward a few months and she became a part of the Photochicks group I belonged to. Photochicks is an amazing sisterhood of friends who are photographers, but also a support network. We get together when we can through the year, but always one weekend a year to end our hectic summer/fall seasons to relax, support, eat, play, sleep and do some fun exercises. Emma is an amazing part of this group offering up her years of photography business techniques, tips and tricks, sharing her little life stories and offering up support to others when we needed it. I would say she's a pretty integral part of our amazing sisterhood network.

I had not been able to go to the Photochicks weekend for three years prior to my first year; My first weekend, was also Emma's first year of Photochicks weekend. We carpooled with our friends Amber and Chelsea, and all the 4-ish hours to Prince Albert County talking about family, life, and Emma's big secret.

That weekend she came out to us, as a medium and empath. I can understand why she felt so nervous. I don't know if you know what a medium is, but I was skeptical. I was so skeptical, my insides were in full blown, "ya right, I loves ya, but I think you're crazy….maybe."

She talked about how as a child she would have 'imaginary' real friends that she would play with, but were really people who had passed on. Growing older she mentions that she spent years of her life struggling with anxiety while trying to suppress and forget about her medium abilities. She goes on to describe that the closer she got back to her mediumship the less anxious she feels. She found and connected with other mediums and joined her Spiritualist Church which helped her exercise her mind and expand upon her Spirit and connecting with Spirits. She then proclaimed that she would do a group reading for the 12 of us that evening.

I had always been a more Spiritual Christian, knowing that and feeling that God is around us and in everything we do, that our ancestors are helping us each day. I grew up with an extended family that used religion as a means of control, ways to judge and condemn. I knew that religion, in that sense of the literal word, was not for me. I always felt close to God but in my own way. This experience that I was about to have with Emma, gave me the confidence that how I felt about my Spirituality and god, was truer than I had ever realized.

As she stood barefoot in front of us, she started off explaining who she is, and what she does. "I am a Medium and an Empath, I feel what Spirit feels and this helps me connect with them to share their messages for you."

She explains that when she connects with Spirit, she sees, hears and feels Spirit. She explains when she sees the Spirit it is in many different forms. Sometimes she can physically see them as if they are sitting next to you; she sees a vision in her mind, almost like looking in a mirror; or the Spirit will give her an images almost like a drawing but in her mind.

She goes on to explain the empath part of her gift. She feels Spirit in a few different ways; Physically, she can take on how the Spirit is feeling. If they are sad, she will feel sad. She may even cry with their sadness. She may even feel like she wants to hug you to express their love for you; Movements, she may also take on some of their movements, if they were a dancer or moved in a certain way, she sometimes will find herself doing that; Characterization, she can physically feel their size, their build, their hair and hands; Clarification, she explains that every time she gets something right from the Spirit, she'll get a tingle down her right hand side where all the hairs stand up on end, and if it is really strong her whole body will do this.

I can see Emma walking up and down with her bare feet, strong, pacing and then standing tall.

She stood there barefoot and explained all of this information and I'm still skeptical. I'm still thinking, the same "whatever" notion inside my head, not in a rude voice, but a curious one.

Then she explains that she cannot promise to connect with a specific Spirit that you are looking to connect with, whomever shows up for you, shows up, and at a group reading, the Spirits with the more urgent messages will usually come forward first, so you might not get your message that time.

For the ones that have a Spirit show up, it might not be someone you think, could be a friend, or loved ones family member, but the message will always be for you.

Emma stood in front of us, turning and drinking her water, and tuning into the Spirits. Closed her eyes, her hands embracing each other, head bowed "they are lining up now."

I'm going to describe for you the part that only pertains to me with this particular group reading, not that the other connections weren't meaningful but that is someone else's business to share and not my story to tell.

Flashing back to the reading that changed everything for me, I will describe this like I'm there in the moment.

I can see Emma walking up and down with her bare feet, strong, pacing and then standing tall. Her eyes are closed as she takes a deep breath, her right hand tucks inside her left and her thumb pinches her thenar space (the space between your index finger and thumb). She is in a meditative stance, the room is quite and she's breathing deep. She lifts her head and looks out at us. "I am having burning feeling in my throat and I'm finding it hard to breath, it's something to do with lungs, maybe lung cancer, He's maybe in his late 50s early 60s and he's tall, balding, but his hands are rough, they are big, he worked with his hands they are very worn"

My heart sank, could this be my Poppy. "Emma, I can take all of that, I think it's my Poppy, Gord"

She looks at me and said "my arm just tingled and I know this is for you, but I know you are skeptical so I'm going to ask him for a common place to describe"

She closed her eyes and bowed her head, her hands automatically embracing one another while she squeezes her thenar space, takes a breath, pauses, nods and opens her eyes.

"He is showing me the woods, and rocks like and escarpment, he's showing me trees by a bungalow, then a path leading up to the bungalow stoop, where you can also walk down beside the house, then he's walking in the front door, off to the front door is a sitting room on the right, but he's going straight and he's walking straight into a kitchen where it turns slightly to the right where there are glass cupboards overhead, he's opening the cupboard and pulling something down for you, little figurines, then he's sitting in a white chair that was right there"

I actually am crying right now typing this, as I cried in that moment.

That was the moment when Emma changed my life. She described my childhood home, and the path one would take to enter my childhood home. It was exactly right, it has changed now but then when I was little and he was there, that is what it was like. Even down to the little glass figurines in the old glass cupboard that I would sneak up to play with.

"Poppy, I exclaimed through tears, I've been waiting so long for you"

I'm not going to go into exact details what his message was for me, but I'll give you the highlights as it was very personal.

When he died, a few days later, I had woken up from a dream and walked out to the kitchen and he was there sitting in a chair, wanting me to sit in another facing him, he motioned me forward. I was walking towards him and he said "Amanda, I want you to give life all you've got, and never....." just as he said "and never" he had stood up to hug me but knocked the chair over and I woke up in my bed. I had been in that place between dreams and asleep where you think you are awake, but you're still asleep.

During this group reading with Emma, I asked her if I could ask Poppy a question and I asked him what the end of his dream message was for me. Emma closing her eyes and opening said

After I spent the first ten minutes with Emma. I realized that I was there for a reason beyond wanting to connect with my mother.

"He wants you to give life all you've got and never let what happened to you in your past, affect your future. You need to not carry that forward, you need to let your walls down and let people in. He loves you so much Amanda, I can feel the love and it's amazing.

She had tears in her eyes.

There was a lot more to the message, but alas it was all for me. It gave me closure for sure but also gave me a whole new perspective on life, Spirituality and death.

Closing the message, Emma stumbled backward, just like Poppy used to, it was so surreal to see her move like he would have. She opened her eyes and tapped her leg like he used to do when he wanted us to sit on his lap and opened her arms for a hug like he used to do, and hugged me (from him).

I was a mess for a while after that, but so very happy.

I decided in that moment, that my friend Emma, The Barefoot Medium, was a gift. She was and is a gift, she's the real deal.

This was a few years ago and over the last few years I've watched her blossom into her Mediumship, she's put herself out there more and more, doing one-on-one sessions, group readings and the latest large group readings at a Monigram Rosters Coffee shop in Cambridge.

I've had a one-on-one with Emma, where my cousins Mark and Jimmy came to give me a message; She didn't know specific things about them before the reading, and knew things she couldn't have known, and my god she's on point. Jimmy protects my heart and Mark is by my side. The message from that meeting was that things were going to get bumpy but just stay the course and it will be okay. If you want to read some of my past blogs you'll see how bumpy that time got.

I highly recommend having a one-on-one session with Emma, it is intimate and the messages are more detailed (as the Spirit doesn't want to get too personal at group readings).

We get together for coffee or chat over the Internets, and I cherish my friendship with her. I get excited when she talks about what she's doing for herself, things she's doing as an amazing mother and how she's nurturing her mediumship more and more.

I wrote this post not just as a testament for her, not just as a friend, but as someone that wants to see her shine, to support and share her with the world. There are many mediums out there, even at the Spiritualist church which I've attended, who are so very talented also, but Emma offers up something unique. True Spiritual empathy and connection. I believe that her ability to connect with Spirit will only get that much stronger as she reaches new milestones along her journey.

I'm honoured to be her friend and I'm thankful for the gifts she's shared with me.

▶ **Sara's Story.** ◀

I went to see Emma in the late summer of 2014. My mother had passed away in 2000 and I longed to have some sort of connection to her. I thought I wanted her to speak through Emma and tell me that I was doing a great job of raising my son. I wanted some affirmation from beyond.

I've always felt like a Spiritual person and I go to see a numerologist every year with my girlfriends, more as a fun weekend away then as a serious visit. I had recommended Emma to my cousin as I had heard she was doing mediumship, and my cousin said it was life changing. I thought, what do I have to lose?

After I spent the first ten minutes with Emma, I realized that I was there for a reason totally beyond wanting to connect with my mother.

As we went to sit down, Emma looked uncomfortable and asked what was wrong with me? She said my energy was completely off and that she could sense I was in a bad place. Then she said, 'are you having some issues with your sister?' I immediately started to cry. My sister, who I've always been crazy close with, had shut me out and wasn't speaking to me. We had recently returned from a vacation together where she hadn't said more than a sentence a day to me and I was devastated. I knew that it stemmed from the fact that she had chosen to move cities and hadn't told me. She was avoiding me.

Emma said, 'you don't need to worry, by the beginning of December, she is going to move cities and the space between you will be necessary for you both to grow and become your own people.' She had no idea that my sister was moving, but I did. This sealed the deal with me that Emma was the real thing within the first five minutes. I called my sister and left her a message after and said, 'so my medium has even told me that you're moving, do you think you can?' A week later she called me back and told me everything. We tearfully made up and the move has been amazing for both of us - just as Emma said.

After that, Emma was able to connect with my mother. Her hair stood up on her arm and she had this smile on her face. 'Wow, she has a lot to say.'... I couldn't stop laughing, that would SO be my mom. She gave me so many messages from my mother that I needed to hear. It was so freeing. I felt a release that I haven't felt since my mother had died. I felt peaceful.

My mom also sent Emma a message about my love life. I have been single for a long time. Right before I went to see Emma, I had a realization that I was falling for a good friend of mine but was afraid to proceed because it was complicated. Emma said, 'your mom said to stop worrying about being single and that you already know who you'll end up with.' She said that I shouldn't be afraid of complications because

I certainly wanted to believe that all their energy didn't just leave this world, that they weren't entirely gone.

every relationship I'd ever had had been complicated and that this wouldn't be any different.' Then Emma described what she thought he was like, physical traits and what he drinks. And she was 100% on. I was stunned as it was really only the week before that I had admitted those feelings to myself and here was Emma describing him to me perfectly.

When I left the reading, I was exhausted. There was so much emotion - tears and smiles. I drove straight to my father's house to talk about some of the things that Emma and I had talked about. He was so skeptical and questioned why I would do something like see a medium. Then I relayed some of the messages that my mom had sent through Emma. Specifically that she wished that she hadn't been so involved in our lives when she had been in them. How that now she can reflect, she wished she had let us make our own mistakes. My dad had always felt that she regretted that and was shocked that that was relayed. He wanted to hear more.

Since I've been to see Emma, I've shared my story with many friends. I think that when you lose someone you love, even if you have a chance to say good-bye like I did with my mother, you need to be reminded that they are still with you. I had felt my mother before very strongly, just once. Now I feel a general comfort because I know her Spirit is still here. I believe it now where before it was only a hope, a dream. Now to me it's a reality. I also think you may not even know the reason that you need to see Emma. I wasn't aware of what I needed to hear until she told me, if that makes sense.

Emma will change your life.

▶   **Tara's Story.**   ◀

My Mother died 4 years ago, she was only 60. When your Mother dies, a part of you dies along with her. It's so hard to think about her, so hard to remember her, so hard to celebrate her life; because you are in so much pain. You busy yourself physically and mentally so that you don't let yourself think about her, because you know if you do, you're going to feel so heartbroken and you're going to have such a huge meltdown, that it will take hours to get over it. To stop this wretched sadness from taking over, I kept myself busy with my young kids, my family and friends, volunteer work, tasks and errands and work around the house. I didn't feel I had time for a huge meltdown or for the long hours of sadness that would settle in afterwards. Even when I was alone, I felt like I couldn't handle the enormous waves of emotion that would wash over me, the overwhelming feelings of missing her so much. It's really unbelievable how I could just push thoughts of her out of my mind. This is how I coped with her death, because I felt like she was gone, gone, gone. I couldn't fathom the idea that everything she worked for, all the energy she spent creating the life that she so desperately wanted, all the love she had for us , all down the drain... what a waste of time, what a crime that she was taken so young, it was so unfair.

After a few years, I start getting scared that I was forgetting details about her. Her voice, her eyes; the way her hands looked. I had been refusing to think about her, because it hurt too much. But then I realized that by doing this, I wasn't honouring her memory, I wasn't talking about her to my children or my brother, and I wasn't sharing memories of her with the people who loved her as much as I did. How to remember her and honour her without having a complete breakdown in front of my children?

My daughters are five and seven. I always wanted to tell them about Mom and sometimes I was able to, but I would start crying or my throat would close up so tightly that I wasn't able to speak properly, so I would tell them about something Mom used to say or do, and then quickly get off the subject. It was very hard to have an actual conversation about Mom, but I knew that I needed to tell them about her, I had to get the words out. I was actually starting to feel that I was robbing them of knowing her, and that I had to gather some kind of strength to keep Mom's memory alive for her granddaughters.

I had been watching mediums on television and I latched onto the idea, because I thought it would be wonderful if our loved ones could really pass over to the "other side", and were somehow still with us and still able to communicate with us. I'm not sure that I believed in heaven or reincarnation, but I certainly wanted to believe that all their energy didn't just leave this world, that they weren't entirely gone.

When my friend Nikki told me about Emma, I was not sceptical of the gift that a medium could have, although I had heard of good ones and not so good ones, and I didn't know anything about Emma. But when Nikki told me about her personal reading and how her grandfather came through, I was intrigued. Soon after, Nikki set up a group reading with myself and several other people that I was acquainted with.

The session began in Nikki's living room. I instantly liked Emma because she didn't come across like a fortune teller or an "airy fairy". I liked how she described her gift and how she shares it, and how she told us stories of her own life and what being a medium was like for her. We were all quite chatty and giggly, and then Emma was ready to get down to business.

She stood in front of us with her bare feet and a big glass of water, and she closed her eyes. She told us to sit back and close our own eyes and take a few deep breaths. I instantly started getting very emotional. I was worried that Mom wouldn't come through, but I was also nervous that she would. Right away Emma said that there was a woman, a mother figure, on her right side. "She is short and has dark wavy thick hair. There is a weight on her chest and a pain across her back..." Oh My God.. I knew it was my Mother, but didn't want to jump in too quickly in case I was wrong. Emma opened her eyes and looked right at me. "Is this someone for you?" she asked. I nodded my head and tears were streaming down my face. Emma told me to say something out loud because my Mom needed to hear my voice. I barely was able to say "Mom, it's me".

Emma then said that we should try to get a shared memory, and there was no denying that it was my Mother when Emma described our house at Christmastime, the most special time for our family. And then all of a sudden, Emma asked if my Mom drank. My Mother certainly drank alcohol and everyone remembered her famous call out at 6:00pm for "Libations!" Nikki and I stared at each other and then burst out laughing. We knew then that it was definitely my Mom!

The messages that Emma gave me from my Mom were not only emotional, validating and comforting, but it reassured me that

Mom is here with me. She is watching over me and taking care of my family. So even though her body isn't here, her Spirit is truly with me and I feel her presence all the time.

Now instead of feeling depressed and sorrowful, I feel excited and happy that she's with me. I have her picture beside me and I talk to her all the time. Because I feel she's here, I don't cry as much, I have the strength to talk about her without getting too upset. I am able to talk about her and share her with my children. We celebrate her all the time, not just on her birthday, but whenever we have a family occasion, whenever we have a memory.

When your loved ones die, the saddest thing in the world is not remembering them. If you don't talk about them out loud, and remember them with your friends and family, they feel like they don't exist, and that maybe you didn't love them as much as they thought you did. But by being able to talk about them, you are showing them how very much they meant to you, and you're validating their existence.

My experience with Emma showed me how to look at death in a different way, to not be so sad about it, to realize that you still have a relationship with your loved one, it's just on a different level. Your Mother is still with you, helping you, guiding you and taking care of you, loving you. You still get to have all of that motherly comfort, even though she's not physically here.

And my Mother likes it too because as she said when Emma did a reading with my whole family, she finally has everyone's attention, and that for once we are all listening to her wise words. She feels even more important and valued than she did when she was here, and she is really excited about that!

Emma has literally changed my life, and my family's life. She has given us peace, and our experience with her has allowed us to further open our hearts to each other. She gave us the ability to remember our Mother, to share our laughter and our tears, and to ensure that our children know her, remember her, and love her, just as much as we do. Thank you Emma!

When I went to see Emma for my personal reading, I didn't quite know what to expect but I knew I was excited and a little nervous about who might come through and what they would tell me. I didn't have much skepticism as I whole-heartedly believe in mediums and that our Spirits cross over. I went into the session with the hopes of hearing from my grandparents, but I wasn't expecting anything specific. I was curious and hoped that maybe someone had a message for me that could perhaps lead me in the right direction, let me know what I was doing in my life was right.

My grandmother and another relative came through with messages for me. The other relative was clear who he was but he mentioned the family reunions he attended at my parents house when I was a child. I received some business advice from him regarding my contracts as a small business owner suggesting I clear up a particular point to avoid being taken advantage of, which was great. I also heard from a friend of my husband's who had exited the world as a teenager. I was amazed. When I returned home and told my husband his friend came through, he looked shocked yet he was happy to hear that his friend watches over him and our family and that his friend is happy to see how Jeff's life is going. I did not know that my husband had a friend die when he was a teenager, so when I was receiving this reading I just wrote everything down and brought it to my husband.

After the reading I felt positive as they solidified my beliefs that when we die, our energy is still here and our loved ones are not gone forever. Not much changed for me after the reading with Emma, but my fears of dying did subside. If you are looking for direction, unanswered questions, or just hoping to hear from a loved one, I very much recommend a reading with Emma. Emma is an amazing medium, the real deal! And although she can't control who comes through and what messages you may receive, she is a vessel that is able to connect you with people who have crossed over who may have something special and important to tell you.

THE GIFT ·

Thank You Emma for helping us by connecting us with loved ones who have left this world.

▶ Melissa's Story. ◀

This past October I received news that my father was in a bee sting accident that resulted in him being in a coma. After multiple tests, and many doctors telling us that his brain would never recover and he would never wake up we made the decision as a family to take him off of life support. I never thought anything like this would ever happen to me, my family or anyone I even personally knew. You hear about random accidents all of the time but never think it will ever happen to you.

Losing my father so suddenly put me in absolute shock, everything happening around me felt so surreal. A few months after the funeral I received a phone call from my friend's mom telling me to come to a group mediumship reading. My friend's mom lost her husband a few years ago and knew that I was always open to anything Spiritual especially if it meant hearing from my dad. I agreed to come to the meeting and was hoping to at the least hear some type of message or have some type of lesson to take away from my dad, Mike.

He was always my number one supporter and inspiration when it came to anything in my life and without him around I felt empty and unmotivated. In my mind I wished for him to show up at the group reading and tell me something that would help inspire me to know he is watching over my family and I, taking care of us. I am a pretty open minded person when it comes to anything along the lines of mediumship but I do have to admit I didn't know what to expect, and had a few small doubts about what I thought it would be like. I also was worried that maybe he wouldn't even show up at all because it had only been a few months since he passed.

When it came time to start the reading Emma did an amazing job at explaining her background, who she is, and most importantly why she does what she does. I find it extremely heart-warming that she chooses to share her gift with people to help bring people a sense of clarity and relief. Right from the start I knew

Emma was genuine because of her introduction. She said she wasn't going to stand there and tell us your loved ones say "I miss you" because of course they do. Then she went on to explaining she is going to try to communicate something deeper and more meaningful than that from whoever it is you were there to connect with. I absolutely love that she said that. During the reading a few people came through that were loved ones of other guests in the room.

I was in awe with the things she was communicating and how people were understanding what she was sharing from others that had passed so clearly. When she started describing my dad I knew right away based on the actions that she had described it was him. He was making a coughing noise as if he was clearing his throat, which was something he always used to do. He stood behind her and she explained what his hair looked like, his height and size.

Emma explained at the start of the reading that sometimes she can physically feel in a way how the person passed and when my dad came through she said her throat felt as if it was closing up. When my dad was stung by the bee he went into anaphylactic shock and couldn't breathe... so that explains why Emma's throat felt as if it was closing. Once she explained all of this I said "that is my dad". I started crying because it wasn't just what she said it was how I felt.

When we came to agreement that it was for sure my dad she had said that he kept showing and talking about a map of Ireland. My parent's traveled a lot and their last trip was to Ireland. They had the time of their lives there. He kept telling me that I needed to go there on my next trip. He said he was so happy that he got to go there with my mom. Another thing that I took away from what she said during the reading was that she pointed out the spot in which I was standing in the hospital when he passed. I held onto a lot of guilt because I was the first person to suggest to take him off of life support because he would never have wanted to live like that. My dad was such a lively person he would have never wanted to have been seen that way, and he would have wanted to been remembered as the outgoing, energetic, happy person that he always was. When she pointed out where I was standing I was listening very carefully because she said he was there with me, and he wants you to know that you don't have to feel guilty for wanting the best for him. He said we made the right decision and at that point he had already made the choice to leave his physical body and cross over.

After hearing all of this I felt so much better. Of course every day is still a process in my grief journey and I miss my dad every day but at least now I know that I don't have to feel guilty. I also know in my heart that he is with me every day and always guiding me through intuition.

In Emma's group reading I found that I learned not only what my dad wanted me to know but a lot more about myself that I didn't know before. I learned to follow that gut feeling that you get when it is there because it is guiding you in the right direction. I learned that it is okay to be happy after losing someone because they want you to be. I learned it is one hundred percent okay to talk to the person you have lost out loud, because they can hear you and if whoever you have lost is like my dad trust me they want the attention. I would recommend Emma to anyone who is wanting to hear from a loved one, friend, or even just see what mediumship is all about. She is caring, has the best sense of humour, and teaches you things you can't learn from anyone else. She is so compassionate and driven with helping you connect with whoever it is you may be looking to talk to.

▼   ▼   ▼

EMMA'S EXERCISE RECAP.

▼

EMMA'S EXERCISE • 1

$\triangledown$

PAY ATTENTION TO THE MAGIC
OF THE PRESENT MOMENT

The magic is all around us. It's the moments of clarity, deja vu, tingly goosebumps- the moments when you think 'That's fucking weird!'. There are always signs pointing us in the right direction. Whether we choose to see them or not is our decision. The signs are everywhere! You have to really work at not seeing them. But we miss them so often because we are not paying attention in the moment. They could be things you are drawn to, the people around you, themes that keep showing up or physical senses or emotions.

Being an empath, many signs for me come from how I feel, physical senses and emotions I pick up. When I pay attention in the moment, I have one particular sign as a medium and an empath, to know if I am on the right track with a client or something I'm working on. It is a distinct tingle (like goosebumps) down my right arm. When I'm on the right track, goosebumps shoot down my arm like a wave.

The lesson here is to pay attention to the little things. The messages are there waiting to be decoded. Be present, in the moment and look around you. What do you see? How do you really feel? If you are ever experiencing anxiety or overwhelm, that is a sign you aren't being present. You are focusing on the past or the future. This takes away your power because you cannot change the past and the future has not yet happened. Stay where you have the power to do something, stay in the now.

Find complete awareness of the very moment you are in. Being present allows you to focus on this very second, on what is happening right now instead of your perception of the past of the perceived future. Be totally and utterly focused on the now.

I would like you to begin a new practice. The practice of being present, 'in the moment'. Here is how I do this daily:

- Put your feet on the floor. Hands on your lap. Now take 5 deep, controlled breaths.

- Draw in that breath all the way down to your toes. Feel it fill you up.

- Note the stress leave your shoulders. Note the texture of the floor under your feet.

- Feel your breath on the back of your throat as you control the flow of it. Breathe in for....1...2...3.... and out for ......1....2.....3.... and in for ....1...2...3.... and out for ......1....2.....3. Repeat this 5 times.

- Now for the next few minutes, try and take in everything around you. Notice what you touch How does it feel? See the light through the window or the trees and the wind on your face. What can you smell? Look slowly around you and take in everything you look at, appreciate its existence. This is where you find clarity. This is where the messages are.

You may not notice too much the first few times you do this, however the more you practise- the more you will allow into your awareness. You may even find some goosebumps along the way. Keep a journal on your 5-10 minute sessions and take note of everything you experience. Watch yourself grow in awareness. It's a beautiful thing.

'Wherever you are, be all there.' — Jim Elliot

EMMA'S EXERCISE • 2

$\triangledown$

REMOVE THE SHIT HELMET AND TAKE A BREATHER. A POSITIVE SELF-TALK BREATHER.

The negative self-talk is only reinforcing one thing- that you have your shit helmet on. This shit helmet has been holding you back far too long. I know it feels safe in there where you can feel certain and sure of yourself but as long as you stay in there, the harder it is to come out.

It's time to take off the helmet, see yourself for who you really are, see the gifts that you have and celebrate them! So I want you to take your hands and feel for the helmet on your head right now. Picture it. What does it look like? What colour, size and shape is it? Now grab a hold of the base (if it's like an astronaut helmet) or the grill (if it's a football helmet). Take a deep breath in and yank it off your head!

Feel the freedom! See all the beauty in your life and all the magical colour and light that shines around you. Take another deep breathe and feel the positive, kind, peaceful words enter your mind.

Set the helmet aside for a little while and write this sentence out 10 times when you wake up and before you go to sleep everyday for the next week. And if you catch yourself thinking a single negative thought- STOP, remove the helmet, grab a pen and piece of paper and WRITE this sentence.

I am a beautiful, creative being, full of wonder for the courageous life ahead of me. I am love and light, and I choose to let Spirit in!

When you can become aware of your shit helmet self-talk, you can begin to change it. Before long, you'll become aware of when you are putting it back on, instead of when you need to take it off. Awareness is a beautiful thing- it can change your life.

NOTES:

EXERCISE RECAP

EMMA'S EXERCISE • 3

▽

HOW DO I REALLY FEEL ABOUT THIS?
WHAT CAN I DO TO CHANGE IT?

Our emotions are our guidance system. Yet we tend to squash our emotions and bury them deep so we don't have to face how we really feel. Then somewhere along the line we emotionally explode and people wonder why the emotional outburst, all of sudden. When truthfully it was rumbling under the surface all along. We need to learn how to listen to our guidance system and what to do with what we find.

This is tough to do at first. Sometimes how we feel is buried deep under layers of lies and stories we've made up but there is beauty in connecting with how we are really feeling. There is honesty, integrity and authenticity. And when you face how you are really feeling, you can actually do something about it.

1. Think of something that has been bothering you, even if you aren't particularly upset or angry about it. Sit down with a pen and paper and write down how you really feel about it. As if no one is ever going to read it, how do you really feel about this bothersome thing? Keep going until you surprise yourself with the answer- then you know you've gone below surface level!

2. Then step away from the feelings you've written down. Think about what you can do to heal from it. Even if you aren't sure yet, what would be one step you could take in order to move forward? Then commit yourself to doing it.

We must express how we are feeling in order to be at peace with it. We don't always need to understand it, merely accept it and do something about it so we can move on. Failing all of that, find a bail of hay and go at it. Worked for me.

NOTES:

_____

_____

_____

_____

_____

_____

_____

_____

_____

_____

_____

_____

_____

_____

_____

_____

_____

EMMA'S EXERCISE • 4

▽

WHAT AM I COMPELLED TO DO TODAY?

There will be many times in your life when you have this gut feeling. About people, a job or career, your lifestyle and everything in between. I believe this gut feeling, your instinct, is your connection to Spirit. And like I said Spirit just gets this shit. So listen to it.

Think back to some of the major experiences in your life, trace back the time and circumstances prior to the experience and you'll find you already had a feeling, a knowing - you just weren't listening to it. So start listening now. Have the courage to give it life, even if what it's telling you is scary. This is your intuition, your instinct guiding you on your path. If you're ever not sure of what to do, sit quiet for a few minutes and ask. Then, don't think- just feel. What do you feel? Which way are you pulled?

Do you ever feel compelled to do something? But your ego (brain/ common sense) takes over?

Do you ever get a feeling about a person you need to talk to or a place you need to go to?

Choose a day. Possibly a day off for your first few times and make all your decisions based on your gut. I bet it takes you somewhere magical.

I challenge you to start listening to your gut everyday. And listen less to your ego. When you feel compelled to do something, go somehwere or say something- do it. Don't hesitate.

Ask yourself as you begin each day, 'What do I feel compelled to do today?'

That is exactly how I ended up where I am today.

NOTES:

_____

_____

_____

_____

_____

_____

_____

_____

_____

_____

_____

_____

_____

_____

_____

EMMA'S EXERCISE • 5

▽

EXPLORE YOUR GIFTS AND FIND SPACE
FOR THEM IN YOUR DAILY LIFE

For a long time, I didn't allow myself to explore the gift I had been given. I had been blocking any purpose for it by not engaging in the joy it could give me to simply explore my connection to the Spirit world. I allowed my shit helmet to block what was a part of me all along. And because I didn't explore it, I didn't believe I really had a gift until I was jolted me awake with a new awareness. I could no longer ignore it. It was through these gifts that I found my purpose.

Ask yourself, what gifts are you ignoring? Whatever is stopping you from exploring these beautiful talents in life, isn't as strong as you think it is. But you have to make a decision to do something different. You have to make a decision to go for it, regardless of what anyone else thinks. Remember, they all have their own shit hemet.

- Write a list of three things that you are gifted at.

Can you sing? Can you do complicated math problems in your head? Can you fix anything without looking at a manual? Can you write? Are you athletic? Are you a great listener?

- Now have a look at all the gifts you have written down.

Can you identify a theme? Are they all about communication, technical skills, comedy, exercise, helping people?

- Make it a daily practise to include one or some of these gifts into your life. Enjoy the magic of your gifts even if only for a moment.

The things you love or are good at are not an accident, and by creating a space to enjoy them, like I did, you'll find a purpose for them.

Find a place for your gifts in your daily life and you'll watch your joy increase.

NOTES:

_____

_____

_____

_____

_____

_____

_____

_____

_____

_____

_____

_____

_____

_____

EMMA'S EXERCISE • 6

$$\triangledown$$

IDENTIFY SOME THEMES IN YOUR LIFE.
EXPLORE THEM AS IDEAS.

Timing is everything, and mostly out of your control. But what is in your control, is your awareness of opportunity and possibility.

Sometimes in life we think we know where we are going, therefore we put our blinders up to everything else. It's amazing what awareness can bring into our lives if we let it. Just like there were themes for me that I couldn't ignore, you have the same- we all do. These themes lead to the lessons that we need to learn, the lessons that will keep showing up as long as we ignore them. So build your awareness around the themes in your life and watch the doorways open up.

Write down some recurring themes in your life. Explore all areas such as relationships, work, passions, money, things you are good at.

Pick one of the themes that you aren't particularly focused on right now and ask these questions...

- why are you choosing to ignore it?

- what would happen if you explored it?

- what is the worst case scenario if you go for it/get help/ figure it out?

- what will or won't happen if you don't?

We are wonderfully creative beings, the only species on the planet that has the critical thinking mental faculty. Use it. Explore, ask yourself tough questions and acknowledge the new awareness. When the time is right, if you are open to it, the opportunity will arise. Just like me and Bill.

NOTES:

_____

_____

_____

_____

_____

_____

_____

_____

_____

_____

_____

_____

_____

_____

EMMA'S EXERCISE • 7

▽

STOP LOOKING FOR THE BIG SIGNS.
PAY ATTENTION TO EVERYTHING.

First of all, you need to trust your gut. If you think it is a sign- it is. Spirit needs us to trust them and ourselves. They are not going to throw a billboard in your face that says "THIS IS A SIGN!" Unless you choose to see the little signs as big billboards. It's all in your perspective.

I think the relationship we foster with Spirit is built on trust. You, trusting yourself and you, trusting Spirit. It's a sort of faith that we are connected, a belief beyond what we can see. I think that's what people truly come to see me for.

Everyone's signs are different. Everyone's gut feeling will be different. You have to tune into what feels right for you. What are your signs? Explore all the little things, see them as signs and notice how often they show up for you.

Start a 'weird shit journal'. Make a list of the odd things you see on the regular.

Are they numbers? An object or symbol? Is it a sound, or something in nature? Or a tingle down your right arm like me?

I see ravens and crows by the dozens, everyday. Without fail. And they just happen to be a symbol of the connection to Spirit and the afterlife. They are also a reminder of the magic around us.

Once you start to notice and trust your signs, Spirit will show you more.

NOTES:

EMMA'S EXERCISE • 8

▽

GRATITUDE IS YOUR GATEWAY TO SPIRIT.

One of the most magical of practises, referred to as gratitude can change your entire perspective on life. Gratitude or the act of feeling grateful for anything expands us in ways we didn't think possible and connects us to Spirit, universal energy. When we truly feel thankful, appreciative and full of love for what we have, who we are and the life inside of us we can find the beauty in everything, even the tough stuff we experience in life.

What I love sharing with people is that Spirit is trying to give us signs and gifts every day in order to move forward. When you can feel grateful for the guidance, you'll build a stronger connection to it. Every time I identify a sign or a message, or take a moment and say out loud, 'THANK YOU!' And every single time I do, I build a bond with my sense of knowing, the trust grows and I cement my belief in my ability to connect with Spirit.

So start small. Set a goal for 90 days to wake up every morning and write what you are grateful for in a daily journal. If you would like to pay it forward then post it online on your social media to inspire others to do the same. Start with the obvious and you'll see each day you'll find more and more wonderful things in your life to feel grateful for.

Here are some ideas you can start with...

I am grateful that I am alive to take on the day!

I am grateful for the ability to see the beautiful world and all it's vibrant colour!

I am grateful for the abundance the universe gives me!

I am grateful for the food in my fridge and the coffee in my cupboard!

You get the point. Starting your day on a positive note shifts your energy. It gives you the awareness of your surroundings and it makes you take notice of and feel grateful for the small things in life. Gratitude is where you can start to truly connect with and let Spirit in.

NOTES:

_____

_____

_____

_____

_____

_____

_____

_____

EMMA'S EXERCISE • 9

▽

HONESTY IS THE BEST POLICY.
WHAT DO YOU REALLY WANT?

Communication with yourself is the most important thing you can do to create peace and abundance in your own life.

Let's start with what is most important to your own Spiritual growth. What are your wants, needs and desires? Do you know? It is in this exploration of desire you will find some hidden meaning, some idea of your purpose and where you should focus in life. But before you do this exercise, I want you to promise yourself that you will be completely honest with yourself.

- Make a list of the top three things you want to achieve in your life. Big scary goals!

- Ask yourself the following questions and be brutally honest with yourself here.

  - Are they your Partner's/Father/Mother/Children's wants, needs or desires?

  - Are they what society thinks you should do, the 'norm' for people in today's economy?

  - Are they what you've already started in life, so it's easier just to continue?

  - Are they limited what you think you can achieve instead of what you really want?

- Now, after reflecting on these goals, write the list again but this time consider the following...

    - If there were no limitations of money/time/effort or societal/family pressure, what would those three things be?

- Lastly, explore why these are important to you. WHY do you want to achieve these goals?

Now you're starting to let Spirit in!

NOTES:

_____

_____

_____

_____

_____

_____

_____

_____

_____

_____

_____

EMMA'S EXERCISE • 10

$\triangledown$

TALK TO YOUR LOVED ONES.
THEY ARE LISTENING.

People think they need to come to me to connect with Spirit. This couldn't be further from the truth. You come to me for validation. But your loved ones are always around you. You can speak to them whenever you like, and they'll hear you. You may not get a response back, at least in the way you want or the way I do, yet. Just know that they are listening.

Talk to them every day. Tell them what you want to say. Tell them how you are feeling and what you are thinking. Picture them with you, around you. Be with them, feel like they are beside you because truly, they aren't that far away.

Spend a little time each day talking to whom ever it is that you would like to engage with. It will feel funny at first, but you'll find a groove with it as the days go on, and maybe you'll even start to see some signs that they hear you!

- Picture your loved one with you having coffee in the morning, or by your side as you drive to work.

- Talk to them about how you feel, what you are thinking, or recount an experience you had with them that brings back fond memories.

- Notice how you feel and what's happening around you. Don't expect a sign back, just pay attention.

Fall in love with the idea that you can talk to them and you'll never think they aren't with you here. Which makes sense, because they never left you in the first place.

NOTES:

_____

_____

_____

_____

_____

_____

_____

_____

_____

_____

_____

_____

_____

SOMETIMES
THE QUESTIONS ARE
COMPLICATED

&

THE ANSWERS ARE
SIMPLE.

– DR. SEUSS

Q & A TIME!

▼

I know you still have questions. I know I didn't really get into how it all works- I'm saving that for the next book. BUT I want to leave you with some of the most common questions I am asked about my mediumship. Mostly because they make me laugh.

Enjoy!

Why doesn't Spirit show up clearly and make it easy. As in "Hi my name is Bob and I'm your dad and you are 37 and drive a pink Jeep."

Spirit needs us to be on board. They need us to work with them and believe that there is a true connection with Spirit. If I were just to give you everything- BAM! It would be overwhelming and your ability to be present and fully receive the message would be unlikely. I find if Spirit eases you into it and includes you in the process, the message is more likely to stick and make more sense to you. I always find a way to validate their presence for you, but some of the detail just isn't necessary- the message is the most important part.

Does Spirit see us all the time? I mean, are they in the shower with me?

I feel that Spirit is with us a lot. And at times when we would probably think it is't a good time. My father-in-law used to sit on the end of my bed at night. But I think they are a polite and much like our physical selves. Would they be in the shower with you you when they were here? I believe they are waiting for the perfect time to connect. Also I don't think they see us as clear cut. It's like a haze. I actually do a lot of my communicating in the shower in the mornings. It's one of the only times I get to myself as a mother of a four year old. And I don't get the feeling they are sneaking a peak, they have much better things to be doing.

My loved one died last week. Will they be able to connect with me?

My friend Carol had the best answer to this question. If their "Spiritual GPS" is set then yes! No problem. My father and I talked about Spiritual things a lot before he passed and even though ultimately I don't think he had an idea of where he was going when he passed, he knew he would be able to communicate with us. And that he did! Minutes after his passing we were sitting with the Trillium Foundation representative and her pager went off to the tune of "Hey Jude" by The Beatles. She was quite embarrassed and said "Who set my pager to that?!" My mum's name is Judith and my dad used to call her Jude. Mum and I just looked at each other and giggled, in unison we looked up to the sky and said Hey Dad/Fred. Then her pager went off a second time and we were convinced, grinning ear to ear. My dad was communicating from the other side.

What if your GPS isn't set when you go? Well, if you had no connection to Spirit/Spirituality/God/Allah/Mother Earth (whatever you want to call it) then it may take you some time to get your coordinates in order. First of all you need to figure out where you are, then you need to realize you can communicate. Then you have to go about finding out a way how to do that so your loved ones will find a way to receive the message. I believe it's the same for learning our connection here in the physical world. Some are more connected than others.

Can I ask questions during our session?

Yes and No. I know. Not very clear, is it? So if I am in a one on one and we have time to get deep down into the nitty gritty of the energy and the connection is really strong. Yes, by all means ask away. If I am at an event and I'm doing speed round sessions and I am trying to get to as many as people as possible then I like to say 'no'. As one of my medium friends Brenda says 'it is a greeting not a reading'. Also, you have to pick your time appropriately. Sometimes I am right in deep with the energy and receiving some important information- interrupting that flow is like snapping an elastic. It brings me right out of the energy and the message can be lost. So I will usually let you know if it is an appropriate time to ask your questions.

Why can't everyone see Spirit the way I do?

Well, as I have mentioned in my book, I think we all see Spirit in our own special way. I am fortunate to have the ability to Feel/ See/Hear/Taste/Smell Spirit. It wasn't always that way though. I've had to work at it and dedicate time and effort to developing my connection with Spirit.

I think we are all on our own journey and each of us has different timing for different reasons. But! I do tell people all the time to disconnect from technology. Go outside, meditate and you will find Spirit everywhere. 1 in 10 people take my advice. And even less stick with it. That is up to you!

Where do you think "heaven" is?

I don't really believe in heaven as a place. I believe it to be more a 'state of consciousness'. I believe that we make our own version of "heaven or hell" based on how we live our life here.

Meaning, if you live a true and authentic life here, give to others freely, don't judge and help guide others down a true path then when you pass over you get to go lay on the beach and drink margaritas. Or that is what I plan to do anyway.

If you lie, cheat, do people wrong and live an unauthentic life based on ego, then when you pass over I think you have to run around and make amends for all the things you did here. And trust me you will spend an eternity doing it because there isn't a medium on every corner, yet :)

Aren't you afraid of Spirit? What about poltergeists or evil Spirits etc.

First of all, I only ever ask for messages for the higher and greater purpose of all.

Secondly, I don't believe in evil Spirits. I think there are evil people that take energy and make it negative.

We are trained from day one to believe that ghosts and Spirit are out to get us.

Trust me, I still sometimes jump under the covers! But only because I am too tired to talk and I don't take time to ask the question "Why are you here?" Ultimately I think that is all Spirit is trying to do. Communicate. And sometimes I need a break.

Look at it like this. If you had a friend and every day you saw them and you tried to tell them that they were headed in the wrong direction and you think they needed to take stock of their lives. If that friend didn't even acknowledge your existence, they even turned way from you, would you sit idly by while they continued to make that mistake or would you throw a book at them or take them by the shoulders and shake them? If you are a good friend, you would do the latter. That is exactly why Spirit gets angry. We don't listen. And then we misinterpret their lashing out.

Do other Medium's give you messages?

Yes, all the time.

One night, I was booked for a meditation group and I had a feeling it was going to be cancelled. Sure enough, it was cancelled and that allowed me to go to the weekly meeting at the Spiritualist Church to give messages. That night at the church, a guy who I've never met before, came up me to afterwards and handed me a message written on a piece of paper from my Dad. It was a goodbye note. That I had made him proud and he could love me from afar. I got the goodbye that I needed since he had slipped into a coma while I was away from the hospital.

This man knew my Dad called me 'Em', he knew that I came from a family of 5, he knew that my mum had miscarried many years ago (in Spirit we always include the miscarriages in the family count) and he knew that our family name was S. And I knew where it was all coming from. The man said that my Dad walked up to him and says 'I know how this works, if I give you a message you have to give it to her." Amazing.

If the meeting hadn't been cancelled and I hadn't gone to the church, I wouldn't have got the message from my dad. But it was all meant to be.

So yes, the answer is a big 'YES!'

DO YOU HAVE THE
COURAGE
TO USE THE
TALENT
YOU WERE
BORN
WITH?

– WOODY ALLEN

AFTERWORD.

▼

WRITTEN BY JUDITH S.

Emma is a determined, driven individual and has been for as long as I can remember. As a child if she wanted something she would plough through any challenge until she reached her goal, prevailing against most of the daunting difficulties she faced. Whether it was joining a sports team at school or learning a new skill; where others would give up she would keep going. So when Emma decided to become a photographer she didn't just want to take photos. She worked really hard at learning the skills required to take amazing photos and consequently, has become an outstanding photographer. She has earned the success she enjoys today and the happiness she creates for others with it.

Photography, however, is a skill Emma has developed as a result of being in touch with something that I can't quite explain. Although I feel that I am open to many aspects of the Spiritual and meta-physical world, for a long time I found myself sceptical that my own daughter could possibly be a Medium. I had suspicions that the 'imaginary' animals and people Emma played with as small child were probably from the Spirit world but I wasn't convinced until a few years ago.

Emma had let me know she was doing readings for people, con-necting them to their loved ones in Spirit. She had offered a read-ing to both her father and me to experience for ourselves the gift she had been sharing with so many others. It opened our eyes. What a gift it was to hear the messages she shared with us that day. I know that her dad found much comfort from the messages he received and he was so proud that his daughter had found her purpose in life.

For me, Emma's gift came to the fore when I needed it most, when the man I loved for over 40 years passed so quickly I wasn't ready to lose him. Emma helped me have a better understanding of the Spirit world. Knowing I could feel him close and connect with him helped make something totally unbearable- just a little bit easier. She gave me some tips and shared messages from him that helped me so much.

Emma's larger-than-life personality has always drawn like-minded people to her and she can easily get people excited about whatever she is passionate about. Now that she has accepted that she is an Empath and a Medium, she is happily sharing her joy and knowledge with the world providing hope, comfort and connection. Things we all truly need. Many of us are searching for deeper meaning and purpose in our lives. We often don't follow our gut or listen to our authentic selves and find as a result that we are still hollow and unfulfilled inside. We struggle to stand up and say "Hey, this is who I am- come and join me on this journey!"

Following our true path takes courage, strength and most importantly the determination to stick with it. And sometimes we need someone to help us do it. With this book and Emma's guidance you too can learn to say "Hey! this is who I am! I too have Spiritual gifts!" Just as she learned to do, with pride and without fear.

Emma's strength is in her ability to help you find your Spiritual path – whether it is as an Empath, Medium, Healer, or simply learning to be in love with yourself and your life. By following the exercises at the end of each chapter, you too can learn how to tap into your true strength and become your authentic self. One step at a time.

Thank you, Emma, for sharing your incredible gift with the world.

Love Mum.

▼   ▼   ▼

ABOUT THE AUTHOR

▼

Emma Smallbone is a teacher at heart. Born in Portsmouth, England she grew up in Ontario, Canada with a thirst for nature, ancient knowledge, and the art of photography. At a young age Emma knew she had a gift, she knew she could see what others couldn't. For a long time, she just didn't know why. The day Emma faced this gift head on and explored its purpose in her life, she found meaning in sharing it with others.

Today, Emma is a messenger. With a vibrant connection to Spirit, she communicates with your loved ones who have passed. And she is here to teach you that you can too! As both an Empath and a Medium, Emma communicates with Spirit in a way that is all her own. Her ability to make sense of and interpret the extraordinary world of Spirit and the afterlife is humbling and engaging.

Emma believes that we are all capable of connecting with Spirit and is on a mission to teach you how in her debut book titled:

'The Barefoot Medium'- Letting Spirit in... one step at a time.'

When she isn't connecting people to Spirit and lost loved ones, Emma is a talented photographer specializing in capturing moments of pure joy and love such as family portraits and weddings. Emma believes her connection to Spirit acts as an intuitive sense with the subject, allowing her to capture the very best picture every time.

Photographer, teacher, motivational speaker, medium and mum. Emma does it all. But the most amazing thing about this humble down to earth gal is that she wants to share all of it with you and in turn, help you find your own Spiritual path to your purpose and let Spirit in... one step at a time.

THE

BAREFOOT
· M E D I U M ·

SPIRITUAL EMPATH & MESSENGER OF LOVE AND LIGHT

Made in the USA
Monee, IL
04 February 2020